Mrs Wilson's Diary

£1.50

R

Mrs Wilson's Diary

Richard Ingrams and John Wells

Illustrated by William Rushton

Private Eye/André Deutsch

Published in Great Britain 1975 by
Private Eye Productions Limited, 34 Greek Street, London W1.
In association with André Deutsch Limited,
105 Great Russell Street, London WC1.

©Pressdram Limited.
SBN 233 96747 8.
"Mrs Wilson's Diary" as serialised in Private Eye.

Designed by Peter Windett.
Printed in Great Britain by H . Daunt & Co. Ltd. Nottingham.

Lord Gnome Writes. . .

In February 1974 Harold Wilson returned to Downing Street as Prime Minister. Since when Mrs Wilson has, in her now famous diary, made an accurate record of the historic developments during the turbulent months that ensued — the Slagheap Affair, Edward Short's momentous friendship with T. Dan Smith, the ennoblement of Marcia Williams — as well as minor diversions like the continuing economic crisis and the Common Market referendum.

Mrs Wilson was much closer to the centre of events than Richard Crossman. Her diary is a unique document, giving us an unparalleled glimpse of history in the making.

You have in your hands a priceless fragment of our island's story, available at a fraction of its real value.

"My clients take the very gravest exception to this disgraceful and abominable travesty."

Rt. Hon. Lord Goodman O.M.

As Hercules in days gone by
Took out his mighty club
And got his rubber kneeler down
To give the floors a scrub.

So now our Harold forth doth go
To clear away the mess
Which Mr Heath hath left behind
For he can do no less.

What man can shirk his country's call?
Though leisure activities beckon
Though tempting sirens lure and wink
He steadfastly must trek on.

So forward, Harold, once again
To purge the stables' filth
Your tiny mandate in your hand
And redistribute the wealth!

The events of the last few days are still a blur in my mind.
I must confess that all along I have been dreading this would
happen. My hope had been that, after a humiliating defeat at the
polls, Harold, in the natural course of things, would have been
stabbed in the back by his colleagues and been replaced by nice
Mr Jenkins, in which event I am certain that the call would have
come from Oxford for Harold to assume the Wardenship of
Goodman College with a peerage and Fellows' Garden thrown in.
Many is the time I have pictured ourselves seated in the eventide
of life in the quiet quad beneath the old elm tree's lofty shade,
while the Chapel bell tolled and Harold, a handkerchief upon his
head, nodded a benign greeting to passing Professors. Alas, alas, it
is not to be.

I first felt queasy shortly after midnight on the Thursday,
when Mr McKenzie's multicoloured swingometer started to rise
to the left. We were seated with Mr Haines, who has replaced
Mr Kaufmann as Harold's press advisor and general factotum,
on the settee in the Josiah Wedgwood TV Lounge of the Huyton
Intercontinental Hotel, and Harold was feeling very tired after an

exhausting day 'shaking the flesh', as Mr Johnson used to call it. He had already enjoyed two bottles of Corsican Sulphuris Sparkling Tonic Wine with added colouring matter and had sent Mr Haines for a third, when Mrs Short's deep and reassuring voice boomed from the set, announcing in proud tones: 'Harold Wilson is marching triumphantly towards Number Ten'. At this, Harold, who was lying full-length on the settee with his tie loosened and his jacket draped untidily over the back of the seat, focussed his eyes on the glittering screen and remarked: 'Oh, my God, not again!'

Even I, who have seen so much of this man, was astonished at the sudden transformation, as the computer predicted on the basis of the data available to it, a five hundred seat majority for the Labour Party. As if galvanised by some dæmonic energy, he sprang to his feet, struck his forehead with the flat of his hand, and fell back on the settee again, uttering a low groan. 'Y'know, Gladys,' he observed, 'third time around the novelty wears off. Even so, it's something to know you're still loved, that the old magic works its spell. Haines!' — at this the obsequious menial, his ragged mackintosh flapping about him, dropped a low bow and tugged at his thinning forelock — 'order a minicab to take us to the polling station, where Mr Wildgoose is waiting to acclaim the victor.'

* * * * *

The following day, after a sleepless night of popping flashbulbs and harsh arclights, we arrived amid scenes of some confusion at London Airport, and were swept in a triumphant motorcade of two minicabs and Mr Haines on his Honda to Transport House. By now, all was in disarray, with Harold's majority hanging by a thread. Despite this, he insisted on going in person for a preliminary reconnaissance of our old home in Downing Street. Imagine my delight, as we climbed over the familiar back garden wall in an attempt to avoid the prying eyes of the Press, to find Inspector Trimfittering waiting in a flowerbed with his burglar's friend clasped at the ready. 'Kung Fu!' he remarked, bringing it down with a sharp crack on the back of Harold's head. We were soon laughing, however, at the misunderstanding, and tiptoed across the muddy lawn to where the sound of music was audible from behind the French windows and the lone figure of Mr Heath could be descried seated at the grand piano, picking out a mournful refrain on the keys.

'Aha! Look at him now!' cried Harold exultantly.
'Oh Heath, where is thy sting? Where is thy victory?'.
At this, Mr Heath looked up from his playing and rushed to the
French windows — installed, I may say, since our occupancy in
the place of the cupboard where Giles's Mammoth Leggo Model
of the Clifton Suspension Bridge was kept — 'Get out, get out!!'
he cried, gesticulating, 'I am still Prime Minister, I have not yet
resigned! Trimfittering, kindly see these people off the premises.'
When the Inspector did not move, favouring us only with a large
wink, Harold bared his teeth in a look of indescribable menace.
'Ha, Heath!' he cried. 'Your hour is come! I have been waiting
for this moment for a long time!' At this Mr Heath gave a banshee
karate cry and sank his teeth in Harold's leg. As the two men
rolled into the tastefully-furnished interior to a wild snarling and
the crash of overturning *objets de vertu* on temporary loan from
Mr Stevas' collection, an inner door splintered to admit the burly
figure of Mr Cyril Smith, the Liberals' jovial anchor man, who
announced that Mr Thorpe was up for grabs and was prepared to
talk turkey if they would 'see him right'.

No, no, I never can return
To scenes of former woe
The moving finger grimly points
We cannot backward go.

Oh Number Ten, within whose walls
We passed those painful years
Thy portal dark I must eschew
Thou awesome vale of tears.

No more, no more I'll step inside
That echoing marble hall
Harold may do so if he wishes
But I shall not do so at all.

It is not often that I put my foot down in any area where
Harold's prerogative holds sway. However, such has been the case
with regard to our official residence. Against my inner promptings
I agreed to accompany Harold on a tour of Number Ten in order
to give instructions to the gentleman from the Ministry of the
Environment about the refurbishing. When I went into our old
bedroom you could have knocked me down with a feather.
Quite apart from the navy blue ceiling, the decor struck me as
quite inappropriate to the setting. 'Look, Harold!' I cried,
pointing at the Trust House Forte-style single bed unit with
bedhead light, radio and television remote control console,
the shoe-polishing tissue, Gideon Bible and Room Service
brochure. 'Look what he has done to our holy of holies!'
'Never mind, dear,' observed Harold, thumbing through the
Yellow Pages on the suitcase rack, 'we will have all this down in
a jiffy. Though I must say I rather fancy these.' He pointed to a
series of Lagonda-Bugatti Queens of the Road vintage motoring
prints, 1908 to 1910.

But it was on opening the toilet door that something inside
me cracked. Gone were the familiar rusty bath, Mr Kaufmann's
denture glass and wig stand, the Inspector's plastic ducks, and the
nasty dent in the Ascot heater caused by Mr Brown practising his
Great Leap Forward. In their place I saw to my horror a curtained
shower unit, a shiny new rowing machine and various male toilet

accessories neatly arranged on the teak loudspeaker unit.
Across the toilet seat itself was a strip of paper, bearing a crossed
anchor motif and the words 'Sanitised for your Convenience by
the Management'. This was too much for me, and under the
influence of some emotion more powerful than I could understand,
I rushed from the room, stifling my sobs with a hanky. I came to,
standing on the pavement, with Harold's reassuring hand on my
shoulder. 'Now then, my dear,' he soothed, 'don't cry. Haines can
get some old stained wallpaper like we used to have. It'll be just
like it always was. The Inspector will tell Haines what to do.'
'No, Harold, no,' I murmured resolutely. 'Never again. I cannot
go back.'

'But Gladys, think one moment,' Harold pleaded,
dismissing the photographers with an irritated gesture.
'A Prime Minister has to live at Number Ten. It is part of history.

Just as the Queen has to live at Balmoral, whether she likes it or not.' 'But Her Majesty is not likely to be thrown out on her neck next week,' I replied, somewhat cruelly, as I now acknowledge. 'Think of the expense of getting Haines to carry it all out again in a few months' time.' 'Yes, yes, yes,' Harold at length agreed, shielding me from the attention of the Press. 'Very well. For the moment we will stay in Lord North Street. But should my majority become enlarged, we may be forced to move.'

Any hope, however, that I might have entertained of disengaging myself from Harold's business life, has been cruelly blighted in recent days. Poor Nimmo has got very elderly, and I was rearranging him in his basket on the night storage heater prior to turning in with a cup of Waitrose Night Drink when the telephone jangled in the bedroom. I snatched it up, not wishing to disturb Harold who was having a pre-bedtime snooze on the rug, and thinking it might be Edna Healey at Number 11 to ask about what day she should put their dustbins out. Instead, a surly voice remarked: 'Listen carefully. We want fifteen million quid for the miners right away.' I shook Harold awake, and heard him groggily responding to the person's further demands, which included the distribution of free food to the poor, a rent freeze, and the public burning of the Industrial Relations Act. 'Yes, yes,' Harold repeated, 'I will send my Mr Foot to whatever rendezvous you care to name. He is a stooping man with white hair and spectacles. He will be carrying a copy of the *Complete Works of Karl Marx*.' Since then the telephone has never stopped ringing at all hours of the day and night with sinister voices making more and more outrageous demands. For the life of me I cannot think what Harold is going to get in return, but he remains calm, puffing at his pipe in bed and studying an old book by a Mr J.J. Rousseau called *The Social Contract*. I think it is something to do with bridge.

Sometimes I find Harold very hard to fathom.
The other morning we were seated at breakfast enjoying a bowl-
ful of Fruit Enriched Alpenstock Muesli from W.H. Smith's,
when Harold, who was reading the *Daily Telegraph*, did what
he calls his 'nose trick' as he was drinking his EuroHag Instant
Chico Substitute. The Inspector slapped him violently on the
back, but it was some time before he was sufficiently recovered
from convulsive chuckles to wipe the tears from his eyes and
remark, 'Poor old Tricky Dick! Look at him now! Eight hundred
thousand dollars of unpaid taxes! This will prove the last straw,
I think. Ha ha, ho ho. You know, Haines' — and here his voice
became solemn — 'we may have our faults in this country of ours,
poor old Reggie Maudling and so forth, but I thank God that we
in the Labour Party have managed to keep our fingers clean of such
taint. I do not wish to boast, but. . . '

'Ahem!' coughed the obsequious general factotum, standing
with a plastic tray behind Harold's chair. 'Perhaps I might draw
your attention to this item in this morning's *Daily Mail*.'
'Do not bother me now, Haines,' Harold snapped. 'I have little
enough time in all conscience. Good God! They've rumbled her
at last!' His mouth fell open in horror as he gaped dumbfounded
at the banner headline: 'WILSON FORGED LETTER SHOCK
HORROR', held out with trembling hand by the obliging
Mr Haines.

'What is it, Harold?' I cried. 'What does this mean?'

'Nothing, nothing, dear,' he snapped angrily, crumpling the
paper into a ball and cramming it into the pocket of his Lambtex
Nautical Dressing Gown. 'Some fresh attempt to smear me by the
Tory Press. Haines, get Arnold Goodman on the phone at once.
Prompt legal action will soon spike their guns. Gladys, if anyone
calls I am incommunicado.' And with this, he stumped upstairs
and shut himself in the mezzanine simulated tiled convenience.

It was only later in the day, when the Inspector had retrieved
the crumpled ball of newspaper from the pocket of Harold's
dressing-gown, hanging behind the bedroom door, that I was able
to hear the full story. It appears that nice Mrs Williams, the cheer-
ful divorced lady of uncertain age, who has been coming in for

many years to do temporary typing work, had bought a slag heap in Lancashire with the help of her brother Tony, Harold's old chum and erstwhile golfing companion, and subsequently sold it to provide much-needed accommodation for the elderly.
I personally could not understand what all the fuss was about, but the Inspector, who was flattening out the crumpled paper with the help of his burglar's friend, grunted gloomily and vouchsafed: 'You mark my words, Madam, you have not heard the last of this by a long chalk. I'd like to see our Mister Houdini get himself out of this one,' which I took to be a reference to Harold's brilliant tactical mind.

'But why?' I queried. 'It is not as if Harold had anything to do with the old slag. This Mr Field is a mere acquaintance from the Burnham Beeches Golf Club.'

I was just arranging some daffs kindly sent round for Easter by Mr Woodrow Wyatt, when the burly figure of Mr Goodman

squeezed through the wide doorway. 'Aha, ahem, these are hard times, Madam,' he observed, proffering a limp hand, and setting down his heavy briefcase on a fragile gilt chair. 'Hard times indeed. I have no doubt that you are most distressed, ahem, by this as it were unhappy turn of circumstances, most distressed. Still, still, Madam' — and here he shook out an enormous red spotted hanky and blew his nose with a loud trumpeting sound — 'the law is a safe refuge in time of trouble. Were this a matter of more import, I would invite your husband to place himself in my hands, but as it is I have given him the name of a little man just off the Tottenham Court Road who will do everything that is necessary I am sure, entirely to your satisfaction.' At this moment, as our friend mopped his perspiring brow and dipped in the briefcase for a boiled sweet, Harold came back from the office in Downing Street. 'Ah, Goodman,' he cried, espying the portly man of the law. 'You have delivered the writs, I trust? We shall hear no more of this.'

'If I may have a word,' observed Mr Goodman, 'speaking without prejudice, there seems to be *prima facie* no case to be made out for libel as far as you yourself are concerned with regard to this piece of property speculation.' 'Reclamation!' shouted Harold in a sudden access of fury. 'Reclamation, Goodman, reclamation, get that word into your thick skull, Mr Self-Styled Fixit!'

Our visitor appeared unperturbed by Harold's astonishing outburst, and raised a plump hand in propitiation. 'Come, come, Sir, there is no need to be agitated. After all, you yourself are in no way involved, and if this ahem typing lady has proved an embarrassment, surely that is easily settled by ahem seeing to it that she is re-deployed in some less conspicuous field.' With this, he swept out, overturning a chest of drawers by the door in the front room, and leaving Harold in a state of white-faced rage.

Alas, Harold's legal manoeuvres, put into motion by Mr Goodman's friend, would not appear to have borne the fruit that might have been expected. The atmosphere has become very fraught, with the Inspector frightening the ladies in the typing pool off their machines in order to examine them with a magnifying glass, and Harold in a funny, jittery state, posing for cheery Easter snaps one moment and being called away to the telephone the next to listen to the protestations of a high-pitched lady caller, whom he attempts in vain to assuage.

Harold continues to be worried about the state of the nation. He has become very irritable at breakfast, and on several occasions Mr Haines our factotum has been reduced to tears by Harold's tetchy remarks about the scrambled egg being overcooked and leathery. Only the other day, I found him weeping silently over the draining board as he scraped away at the burnt areas of a piece of Sunblest Ready Sliced Calory Reduced Bounciloaf. Apparently Harold, already disgruntled by the leaves floating in the tea, exploded with rage on catching sight yet again of the bouffant hair-do of Mr Millhouse, the Insurance Salesman with a taste for exotic living, this time pictured in *The Times* in a latex jump suit, ski-ing over his wife's watery grave Black Spot. He had rolled the paper into a truncheon and had struck Mr Haines with it, knocking off his reading glasses and causing him to expectorate the mint he was sucking, which fell on the floor and became covered with fluff.

Meanwhile Harold's nocturnal behaviour has been most irregular. He has taken to throwing the clothes off in a violent manner in the small hours, and pacing up and down the room like a caged beast, muttering to himself and clutching at his hair. Last Tuesday I awoke suddenly to find the hands of the Mickey Mouse Luminous Bedside Novelticlock at half past three, and Harold's side of the bed empty and cold. Anxious lest something had happened to him, I put on my Bunnywarm Boudoir Wrap and Dr Scholl feather moccasins, and tiptoed downstairs.

Imagine my surprise to see a bar of light beneath the door of Harold's den, and to hear his agitated voice engaged in conversation on the telephone. 'I am not being hysterical,' he was remarking in a tense shout. 'I am merely stating the facts.' After this there was a long silence, punctuated only by Harold's occasional grunt. Then he said, 'Kindly let me speak. You have had your say.' There was another long silence, during which I could hear what sounded like Harold's foot tapping agitatedly against the Roses of England wastepaper basket. At last he was able to cut in: 'I fully appreciate your desire to build a hedge against inflation,' he observed, 'but is there any more of this dirt under the carpet? Because if there is. . . ' Once again he fell silent in mid-sentence, and the other speaker engaged his attention for some minutes. Finally, his voice unnaturally high-pitched, he cried: 'Just get this straight once and for all. I will not have you conducting your affairs in my office.' With this he slammed down the telephone, which immediately began to ring once more, and another long conversation followed, in which Harold took no part, except to conclude it with the words: 'If that is the way you feel, goodnight.'

I was about to creep away, when the door flew open, and Harold stood revealed, his hair ruffled, his face drawn,

and a wild glint in his eye. 'Ha!' he cried in Shakespearean tone, as I stood transfixed in the beam of light. 'A rat in the arras! What does this mean, Gladys? You are all the same, you women! Can't leave a man alone for a moment!'

'Come now, Harold,' I soothed, 'just tell me what it is that is worrying you. It is better if we have things out.' 'You are right, Gladys, for once,' he riposted, and took from inside his dressing-gown a Four Star VIP Vintage Sanatogen Flask with screw-on silver-style beaker attached, to pour himself a large measure of the amber beverage. He gulped it down, smacked his lips, and repeated the process three or four times before he finally spoke. 'I will tell you the truth, Gladys,' he said. 'That was Jim Callaghan from Brussels. Owing to the time-lag it is the afternoon over there. Naturally he is agitated about renegotiating the terms. I have done my best to calm him down, but he is an excitable person, as well you know.' At this the telephone rang again. 'Aha,' he vouchsafed, 'that will be Brian Faulkner from Northern Ireland with the casualty figures. Go to bed now, Gladys, this will be a long one.'

The same jittery mood has been apparent throughout the routine comings and goings of life at Lord North Street. Mr Benn came round yesterday morning for a few Rondello Cocosnaps and a cup of EuroHag to talk about his plans for nationalising British Leyland at a cost of only £800,000,000,000. 'All set for a June election', he cried as he was going, giving me a gentlemanly peck on the cheek, 'before we get any deeper into it. . . ' 'What do you mean, Benn?' Harold snapped. 'You have been reading the lies and seamy smears of the Tory Gutter Press!'

'Oh no, I assure you,' cried Mr Benn, his eyes popping out with surprise. 'I was thinking of the old bugbear of inflation, to be sure.' 'Poppycock, Benn, poppycock!' Harold countered, thrusting the stem of his pipe up Mr Benn's quivering nostril. 'You would like to see me gone, just like the rest. Get out before I call a policeman!'

As I write, Harold has crawled through the room on all fours, a segment of carpet clenched between his teeth, attempting to avoid the prying eyes of the 'media vultures', as he calls them. If this behaviour continues I may have to have a word with Doctor Melrose.

17th MAY 1974

I always thought nice Mr Short, the stooping grey-haired gentleman and former schoolmaster who was kind enough to un-block our drains when they became clogged with leaves in the autumn, would be the very last person to become enmeshed in what Harold calls the 'Tory muck-rake'. But so it appears, from the events of recent days, is the case.

To celebrate his appointment of a Royal Commission to investigate the sad decline of editorial standards, Harold had asked me to invite Denis and Edna in from next door for a *fondue* party, at which it was our intention to christen a special *fondue* set which Denis brought back from Switzerland as a gift from Herr Edelweiss, one of the famous Gnomes of Zurich. Harold also suggested that Edward and Jennie Short should be asked as well — as the set has six *lippen-skalder* roastiprong forks — and I had asked Mr Haines to bring around half a dozen Pipkins of Wincarnis Corsican Variety from Waitrose.

The fat was nicely sizzling over the methylated syrup stove, and we had all immersed our instruments into the bubbling fluid, when Mr Short, who had been in a thirsty mood all evening, asked if Harold would mind if he switched on the TV to see the Cup Final Late Score on the news. No sooner said than done! Mr Honeycombe's bald pated visage was glistening benignly on the screen, reporting to our great astonishment that Mr T. Dan Smith, the Northern Philanthropist, had donated two hundred and fifty pounds to Mr Short for services rendered. Mr Short had just extracted his fork, wrapped in a hankie, from the boiling fat, and placed the steaming morsel in his mouth. As Mr Honeycombe pronounced the fatal words however, he clapped his hand to his lips, dropping the fork, and uttered a muffled cry of mingled pain and indignation. To make matters worse, the hot fork became embedded in Edna Healey's foot, causing her to hop about in some consternation.

Harold immediately sprang up from his chair, where he had been chewing thoughtfully on a piece of raw meat — as he has never striven to conceal his distaste for what he calls 'this silly foreign *fondue* nonsense' — and switched off the set. Then, his face white with rage, he whirled about and confronted the erstwhile pedagogue. 'What is this, Short?' he cried,

gesturing with his fork at the dwindling image of Mr Honeycombe.
'So you too have had your feet in the trough all along. I might
have known that you were buttering your pockets, along with the
rest of them!' At this, Mr Short removed the charred and still
smoking morsel from his mouth, and speaking with some
difficulty, made some biblical reference to motes and beams which
I was not entirely able to make out. Harold sprang forward,
seized him by the lapels and shouted: 'Just what are you suggesting, Mr Chips?' 'Well,' spluttered Mr Short, attempting to cool
his scalded tongue in a glass of Wincarnis. 'People in glass
houses. . . ' 'Yes?' Harold interposed. 'Go on, go on!'
Mr Short drew himself up and exclaimed, 'If I am to be censured
for a paltry indiscretion involving a mere two hundred and fifty
pounds, I would remind you of the considerably larger amounts
which have been acquired by certain self-styled reclamationists
not wholly unconnected with yourself!'

For a moment Harold appeared thoughtful, and his grip
loosened on Mr Short's shiny Montague Burton-style two-piece
suiting. In the silence that followed, Harold replenished the
glasses in our trembling hands, and himself consumed the
remainder of one unfinished pipkin at a single draught.
'Well, Ted, old chum,' he vouchsafed at last. 'Let us confess there
have been faults on both sides. No-one can be in doubt', — and

at this his voice attained a note of Churchillian defiance as he
swayed lightly on his feet — 'as to who are the true villains of
this piece. I refer of course to the malevolent Tory media,
who, with their vile smears and dirty innuendoes, seek to destroy
the fabric of the People's Government. 'Yes!' cried Mr Short.
'That is what I have said all along. I have heard from reliable
sources that the BBC have offered a five figure sum to the misguided genius T. Dan Smith to spill the beans — I mean to
vilify a top-ranking minister. So this is our Gethsemane,
Brother!'

The scene had become most emotional, with Edna Healey
still sobbing over her wounded foot and Denis weeping softly into
a large white handkerchief. Harold was about to speak, when the
door flew open to reveal the windswept figure of Mr Foot, his
white locks fluttering behind him and his silver-knobbed cane
waving wildly in the air, a number of dusty volumes clutched
under one arm. 'Ha!' he cried, with outstretched arm.
'Who will rid me of this stiff-necked judge, this popinjay Daniel
come unstuck at judgement?' 'Eh?' enquired Harold with a
puzzled frown. 'Cut out the Speakers' Corner stuff, Footy,
and give us the dirt. What's cooking?' Mr Foot proceeded to
launch into an extravagant harangue, of which the gist appeared
to be that unless sixty-five thousand pounds were forthcoming,
Mr Scanlon would bring the country swiftly to a halt.
'A pretty pass, a pretty pass. That I should live to see this!' he
concluded, upsetting the *fondue* pot into Mrs Short's open
handbag with a flourish of his cane.

The matter was soon settled, however, when Harold announced that he would telephone a big reclamation man he knew,
called Mr Field, who he was sure would see his way clear to
contributing the entire sum anonymously from philanthropic
motives.

31st MAY 1974

My fears with regard to Harold's mental health have alas been proved all too well-founded by the events of recent days. The Inspector, who has just returned from a Poulson Package Tour to Malta looking bronzed and fit, first set my mind working when he opened the *Daily Telegraph* and began to roar with laughter. 'Aha,' he remarked, amid convulsive paroxysms, 'now he's gone over the top. Ha ha ha, fancy making a fool of himself at his age! This is really rich, Madam, if you'll pardon my language. Oh, they're not going to forget this one in a hurry, you mark my words!' 'What is it, Inspector?' I queried, as our bodyguard slapped his thigh once more and wiped his eyes with his handkerchief. Seized by a new gale of mirth, he could only point helplessly at the newspaper's headline: 'Life Peerage for Marcia Shock: Consul's Horse Remarks Conservative'.

Imagine my surprise, on perusing the journal, to learn that the Marcia referred to was none other than Mrs Williams, the businesslike divorced lady who has been coming in over the years to help out with the typing. I must say that it came as startling news to learn that Harold had ennobled her, and that she would now be able to take her seat in the Upper Chamber, attired in ermine robes, with a fluffy crown-style hat adorned with golden balls. I was still musing on the revelation, with my arms in the suds washing up after breakfast, when Harold appeared at my side, and placed a thoughtful hand on my shoulder. 'Gladys, dear,' he soothed, 'there is something I feel I ought to tell you.' 'Would you like me to leave, Sir and Madam?' asked the Inspector pointedly from behind his newspaper, his shoulders shaking with silent mirth. 'No, no, Inspector, that is quite alright. Gladys, you are familiar with Mrs Williams, the typing lady, who has been coming in and out these twenty long years? Well, in view of services rendered' — at this the Inspector, to my surprise, suddenly fell off his chair and rolled silently under the draining board — 'and years of devoted help behind the scenes, I have decided that she should receive some small reward as a token of our esteem and gratitude.' 'But what about the slag?' I enquired. 'Was there not some stain, some questions left unanswered?' 'Gladys!' Harold riposted angrily. 'I am surprised that at this moment in time you of all people should give credence to the lying smears of the gutter press.

This will show them who is master now. They may sneer, they
may snigger behind their hands, but what can they do?
All power is mine. I thumb my nose at them. I cock a snook at
the Tory Barons of the Media. Aitken, Harmsworth, Murdoch,
paper tigers every one.'

Harold's voice had by now risen to a shrill scream,
when there came a shy ra-ta-tat at the door, followed by a defer-
ential cough, and Mr Haines, his habitual mint bulging in one
cheek, shuffled in in his green baize apron. 'Well, Haines?'
asked Harold. 'What is it now? I will not have my privacy
intruded upon.' 'May I speak freely?' Mr Haines enquired.
'Like others, I have read this morning's papers.'
'Yes, and what of it?' snapped Harold, peering intently at the

factotum. 'Well, Sir,' the latter quavered, sucking nervously at his sweet, 'in view of the great honour which has been conferred on my colleague, I would respectfully submit that I wish in future to be known as Sir Joseph Haines, Bart. of Clapton. Nothing less will suffice. Excuse me, Sir, I hear someone at the door.'

Harold's face was still purpling with rage when a small bespectacled man stepped smilingly into the kitchen.
'Vot iss diss prize-giving howsyourfather? Vy I ham not inform-ed?' 'Kagan!' Harold replied sharply. 'Kindly use the tradesmen's entrance and confine your visits to the hours of darkness. Gladys, you will no doubt remember Mr Kagan, the gents' haberdasher from Halifax, inventor of the Gannex Raincoat? Well Joey, what are you after now?' 'Ven do I get mein Lordship already? Loyalty, blood, everyting I heff given. Ent now, a slepp in ze face viz a piece of fish. Zis is my reward.'
At this, he burst into floods of tears, and began to paw at Harold's lapels, fingering the cloth with expert hands. Before Harold could detach himself, the telephone rang, and he snatched it up with some annoyance. 'Kaufmann?' he cried. 'No, you may not style yourself Baron Ardwick of Birmingham! Lord Baldilocks, perhaps. Ha ha. No, no. That was a joke. Pull yourself together, man. Stop weeping.'

Mr Kagan's middle European lamentations were still ming-ling with those audible from the other end of the telephone, when a sepulchral voice from beneath the sink announced in booming tones, 'My Lords, Ladies and Gentlemen, pray silence for His Serene Highness, the Markgrave Trimfitting of that Ilk, Lord of the Seven Marches, Grand Master of the Most Worshipful Order of the Bath, Warden of the Imperial Convenience. . . ' 'Enough!' cried Harold angrily to the Inspector who had emerged from underneath the draining board with the pig bin balanced precariously on his head and a wet mop in one hand. 'I will not have my Lady Forkbender's name held up to ridicule. Kagan, back to your raincoat factory this instant! Kaufmann, have a good blow and change your trousers' — at this he slammed down the receiver — 'and Haines! Any more of your lip and you'll be back on the street. And now leave me alone, all of you; events in Ulster have reached boiling point. Roy Mason is bicycling round from the Ministry of Defence to coach me on my low-profile posture.'

O Ireland, so-called Emerald Isle
  Who can thy secrets know?
Where fairies dance o'er rock-strewn pile
  And wand'ring tinkers go.

How bloody is thy destiny
  How full of war thy fate
The conflict and disharmony
  Say, will it ne'er abate?

Alas, alack, the raven cries
  I fear the answer's never;
No Englishman, however wise
  Thy Gordian Knot can sever!

Come Merlyn Rees, thy magic spell
  Weave o'er the blood-splasht peat
And bring those men who now rebel
  Disarmed to Harold's feet.

I wrote these lines sitting on the beach in Gunter's Cove, the attractive litter-free precinct in the Scilly Isles that lies within a stone's throw of the picture windows of our bungalow. In the serene atmosphere of a warm summer afternoon it seemed impossible that terrible fighting and bloodshed should be going on only a few hundred yards away in our back sitting room. But such, alas, was the case.

The trouble began when, following the IRA death threat to nice Mr Jenkins, the Inspector on his own initiative decided to intensify security precautions with regard to Harold's person. Harold did not at first object when he erected an army-style camp bed in our bedroom and dozed watchfully upon it through the hours of darkness with a twelve-bore shotgun folded in his arms. However, when Harold announced his intention, after breakfast, of retiring to the toilet with a copy of *Amateur Detective*, the Inspector's immediate insistence on accompanying him into the tiny cubicle with his loaded fowling piece elicited a sharp rebuff. 'Inspector,' he observed with dignity, his hand on the door of the convenience, 'there is such a thing as privacy.

I have more than enough to put up with, as it is, God knows — the prying eyes of the media and the Peeping Toms of the gutter press — without your mounting a so-called massive security operation of this kind.' 'As you wish, Squire,' the Inspector replied, 'I am only carrying out the Home Secretary's personal recommendations. I shall remain outside the door. But have no fear! If you do not emerge within a reasonable time, I shall break the door down instantly.'

At this, Harold, whose tetchiness has become increasingly marked in recent days, seized hold of the Inspector's shotgun, and closing both eyes, squeezed the trigger, producing a violent explosion and discharging a volley of lead shot into the Habitat inflatable sofa, which began to subside in a sad manner. Sporadic fighting continued throughout the day, causing me to withdraw to the seclusion of the Cove, where I could commune with sea and sky and listen to the mournful crying of the gulls and gannecks.

Harold, of late, has become more and more preoccupied with a large chart which he has, with the assistance of Mr Haines, sellotaped to the wall of his den in Lord North Street. I first became aware of this when Mr Rees, the quiet-spoken Secretary of State for Northern Ireland, came round after tea one day with a harassed look on his kindly, bespectacled face, to ask Harold's advice about what to do next. As Harold had expressed the wish not to be disturbed, I chatted to Mr Rees myself over the gas-stove, and made a good strong pot of Old Baloghi Turkish Tea in an attempt to calm him, suggesting that perhaps the time had come for a reappraisal of the options in the light of the latest developments. Mr Rees listened with great politeness, writing my suggestions down on the back of an envelope, and promising to put them before Mr Paisley when next they met.

At this moment the door of the den was flung open, and Harold emerged, his face wreathed in smiles. 'My dear!' I cried, 'Here is Mr Rees, come to discuss the critical situation in Ireland.' 'Do not bother me with that, woman,' Harold riposted, leading us both into his sanctum with a proprietorial air, 'those spongers across the water have dug their own bed and now they can lie in it. Allow me to introduce the distinguished Television Twins, Mr Horace and Norris McWhirter, editors in chief of the world-famous Guinness Book of Records.' At this, two identical gentlemen in blue blazers and grey flannel shorts rose from the sofa and smiled a wordless greeting. 'This is it!' Harold cried, pointing to the wall-chart, still held in place by a wobbling Mr Haines, perched precariously on the up-turned Roses of England wastepaper basket, itself balanced on a fragile gilt chair. 'Gladys! Rees! Examine this chart and tell me whose is the longest.'

I looked at the chart carefully, and saw the names of all the Prime Ministers of this country since 1900, neatly set out down the left-hand side of a large piece of graph paper. 'Note the lines,' Harold cried. 'Against each name you will observe a strip of coloured tape, denoting the length of tenure achieved by each incumbent. Heath's, as you see, is derisory. Likewise his predecessors': Home's, Eden's, Bonar Law's, all miniscule.

Consider Clement Attlee, a little better perhaps, but nothing to write home about. Only three giants survive your scrutiny: Asquith, Churchill, and myself. Now, I ask you all, what advantage do I have over the two last-named?' Mr Rees assumed an expression of earnest concentration and looked at the ceiling whilst I racked my brains for the correct answer.

'I am sorry,' Harold remarked at length, slamming his fist down on a bell beside his blotter, and turning in triumph to the shyly smiling twins, 'your time is up. Tell them, Haines.'

The factotum turned his head with an expression of eager compliance, and then unfortunately lost his balance and slid slowly down the wall with a cry, tearing a wide swathe of paper from the centre of the chart and disappearing behind the sofa.

'I will ignore that,' Harold observed with dignity. 'The answer is that I am still alive, and that in approximately two years' time I shall surge into the lead, thus meriting inclusion in Messrs McWhirters' Almanack under the category of Longest Serving Prime Minister of the Twentieth Century.'

There was a long silence, broken only by Mr Haines' low moans as he fumbled for his spectacles beneath the tattered remnants of the chart. 'Ahem,' coughed Mr Rees at last, 'how very, very interesting indeed. And now, Sir, if you have a moment, I would be grateful if we could perhaps discuss our policies with regard to the new situation in Ulster. . . '

'Rees!' Harold cried in a sudden access of fury. 'If you have no concept of priorities, you have no place here at this moment in time. Get up Haines. You do not need your spectacles to show Mr Rees the door. Gladys, the Sellotape from the bathroom cabinet and some scissors. This chart must be repaired at once.'

I am glad to say that this has now been done, and it is Mr Haines' task to advance Harold's tape by a centimetre for every week that passes. No visitor is allowed to leave the house without having seen it, and every evening after dinner, Harold sits in front of it with a tumbler of Old Boney Cognac-style Wincarnis, watching it with a glazed expression of contentment on his rubicund face.

28th JUNE 1974

Summer is here, the drowsy heat
O'erpowers each human breast
The bees crawl up the garden seat
Where Nimmo takes his rest.

O glorious June, the long hot days
It seems will never cease
The roses shimmer in the haze
All Nature is at peace.

Now in the equinoxious calm
How hard it is to concentrate
We feel as if we could come to no harm
When in the shade it is seventy-eight.

A strange *ennui*, as Mr Jenkins calls it, has fallen over the house at Lord North Street during these last few glorious summer days. Harold has taken a deck chair right down to the bottom of the garden by the compost heap, and told Mr Haines to inform all callers that he is in a conference, and not on any account to be disturbed. It is my task to replenish his jug of Wincarnis '48D' Cup at regular intervals. He is clad in khaki shorts and sandals, and from time to time applies a generous blob of Kiwi Deep Tan Suncreme, rubbing it lethargically over his pectoral areas.

Unhappily it has proved impossible to protect Harold from all those interlopers seeking to gain access. The other day, I was just helping Haines to put out the Westminster Council Plastibags for the dustmen, when Mr Benn came running down the street, pushing his electric golf car. 'Good day, good day!' he shouted, removing his pipe from his mouth, and treating us to a wide smile. 'And good day to you, Comrade Haines. I have with me my new blueprint for the next thousand years.' At this he extracted from the back of his pollution-free conveyance a massive concertina file, bulging with computerised documents. 'I am sorry,' I began, 'Harold is in a vital conference.' 'That's funny,' riposted Mr Benn, jumping up and down to look over the wall, 'then who is the recumbent figure I can see clearly communing with nature by the rubbish dump?' And before I could restrain him, he leaped over the wall with youthful grace, landing, it seemed, in the Inspector's melon frame.

The resulting sound disturbed Harold's slumbers, and I heard his angry tones calling for the Inspector, announcing that the seat of government had been attacked by the men of violence. While Haines rushed through the house to do what he could, I got out the Instant Wincarnis Powder, and in a jiffy was carrying a tinkling tray, replete with jumbo ice cubes and Haddock'n'Smoke flavour twiglets, down the garden to where the two pillars of the state confronted each other across the steaming compost. Mr Benn had by this time laid out some diagrams on the lawn, which were being earnestly studied by the Inspector and Mr Haines. 'Now,' Mr Benn was saying with serious mien, 'let us take Rothschild's Merchant Bank. All my calculations suggest that workers' control would be bound to ensure a one hundred per cent efficiency increase, allied to a vast growth in international confidence. . . '

'Wait a minute,' cried Harold, turning up the volume control of the Kamikaze Nipponette Dance Special transistor, 'we are just going to get the results of the Peru v Iceland Elimination Replay. Write it down, Inspector! Use one of those bits of paper lying on the grass. Peru 3, Iceland 1 . . . Now Benn, what is this nonsense? Can you not see that I have better things to occupy my mind?' 'Well, Sir,' Mr Benn parried, trying to extract another document from Haines' urgently enquiring grasp, 'this is no more than was set out in our manifesto as approved by conference. . . ' 'Benn,' Harold cried. 'You are no doubt aware of the paper shortage. Haines, recycle Mr Benn's blueprints on the compost heap and give them a generous douse of Fisons' Instirot Liquid Drench. You will see, Benn, old country ways have still much to teach the modern technologist.'

As Mr Benn began to struggle silently over the compost heap with Haines and the Inspector, an executive helicopter puttered out of the blue sky and came to hover a few feet over the lawn, flattening out the flowers in its slipstream and setting Mr Benn's papers once again a-whirling. A nylon rope ladder was lowered, and the figure of Mr Campbell Adamson of the CBI, wearing sunglasses and a para-military bowler hat, was seen descending. 'Ah, Prime Minister,' he remarked in urbane tones, 'I am sorry to disturb your paper chase, but as the Index is sliding so alarmingly and the country's economy is so near collapse, I deemed it prudent to seek an interview with you at the earliest opportunity.' 'Just one moment!' cried Harold, above the roar of the spinning blades. 'Inspector, have your pencil ready! Uruguay 4, Bulgaria 1. Adamson, Mr Foot I am sure will deal with whatever little queries that you have to raise. You will find him in the Reading Room of the British Museum. Gladys, as I seem unable to get any work done here, I have decided to pay a lightning visit to Herr Schmidt, the new strong man of Europe. We have many matters to discuss that could affect the future of the World.'

I was rather surprised, later in the day, to see Harold on *News at Ten*, ensconced in the VIP Box at the World Cup Stadium, sharing what the cameras showed to be a crate of Auld Jock Wincarnie Drink with Mr Hamish McPissartist, Chairman of the Ross and Cromarty Football Hooligans Club, and remarking to the interviewer that he knew more about football than he did about politics, and that everyone knew the date of the election except for him, at which he laughed an immoderate amount and fell out of sight.

Harold remains very relaxed as the slow days of summer progress. Many people have been good enough to call at the house or to phone up, enquiring about his state of health. Mr Mogg, the kind bespectacled former clergyman with the unfortunate speech impediment who edits *The Times*, rang in person as I was unfreezing the broccoli tips to ask if it was true, as he had been informed by an impeccable source at the Conservative Party Central Office, that Harold was a martyr to terminal flatulence and that he was not long for this world. I was able to reassure him, explaining that Harold had only wrenched his knee and developed a fluid intake condition. I did not mention the circumstances in which the painful condition had originated, namely Harold's slipping up in the polished hallway at Lord North Street on one of Mr Haines's mints which he had spat out before opening the door to Lady Forkbender.

Harold's suntrap patio lounge at the back of the house, ingeniously fabricated by the Inspector out of corrugated Perspitex weather sheeting from a plan in the *TV Times*, is now much enhanced by the Mickey Mouse Kiddipool Mini-Marina, kindly donated by Sir Joseph Kagan, the benevolent industrialist from Halifax to whom we owe so much.

Harold finds it eases his knee to lie with his arms and legs draped over the circular framework of the pool, and Mr Haines has arranged the television set on a pulley system somewhat reminiscent of Mr Heath Robinson's labour-saving devices in the 'thirties. Harold has only to pull on a ring to operate a series of cogs and levers which in turn adjust the brightness and contrast knobs for the Wimbledon.

It was thus that Mr Harold Lever found him last week watching the exuberant Mrs Morozova capering with great expert-ise on the centre court, arousing happy memories of our walking-out days at Widnes. 'Prime Minister,' Mr Lever began, adjusting his heavy spectacles on his nose and looking with some curiosity at the Present From Clovelly Novelty Glass containing Cornish Wincarnimeed Summer Drink, garnished with vegetables and made from an authentic Anglo-Saxon recipe over a hundred years old. 'I come hot-foot, or rather, to be more truthful, by chauffeur-driven limousine, from the City. My friends there, worthy men,

interested only in the future of this country, are considerably dis-
heartened by some of the wildcat talk that's going about on the
subject of skinning the rich. They are throwing them out of their
hospitals now, who knows where they will be throwing them out
of next week? Normally sober voices' — at this Mr Lever took a
tentative gulp of the Cornish Liqueur and registered a strange
expression of moral distaste mingled with surprise on his face —
'in board-rooms, Turkish Baths and five star restaurants are
talking seriously of suicide. It cannot go on, I tell you. Business is
business. What with this Healey lunatic and now this Benn, it'll
be a bloody revolution already.' And with this he spread his hands
in a gesture of entrepreneurial despair.

Harold gazed up at him from the cooling waters with a
glazed expression on his face. 'You are quite right, Lever,' he
vouchsafed at length, delving beneath him for a chilled bottle of
Sanato Spumante and wiping his hands absent-mindedly on
Mr Lever's pin-striped trousering, 'the wild men of the Left
have had their say. It is a time for common sense and moderation.
Go back now, Lever, and tell your friends and brethren there
within the Sacred Mile that we are fully aware of the burdens
under which they labour. They cannot make bricks without
straw. They are our golden geese, the lynch-pin of our very way
of life, merchant venturers. . . You can speak their language,
Lever.' At this, Harold's voice became unnaturally quiet, so that
Mr Lever was obliged to bend over lower to catch the precious
words. 'Go, dear Lever,' observed Harold, caressing Mr Lever's
curly locks in a paternal manner, 'go tell the merchants, the
money-lenders, the publicans and sinners that I am one of them.
I will not leave them nor desert them at this moment in time.'
Mr Lever appeared satisfied with this somewhat emotional outburst, and taking his shiny top-hat from Mr Haines's obedient
hands, he made an excuse and left.

He had been gone but a moment when the sound of a silver-
knobbed stick beating on the panel of the front door aroused me
once again from my television reverie. I opened the door to dis-
cover Mr Foot, wearing, despite the summer heat, an ancient cloak
and bearing in his hand a calf-skin folio entitled *Boggins's Rights
of Man or Mercantilism Explained, 1788.* 'Good day, my dear
lady,' he remarked, sweeping a low bow, and without further ado,
strode purposefully through the dark hallway towards the sunlit
patio, where the quiet *wock-wock* of the tennis balls supplied a
soothing rhythm to Harold's meditation. 'Advantage Miss Rostro-
povich,' a voice announced as Mr Foot arrived at the edge of the

mini-pool, eyeing its occupant with ill-concealed disgust.

'Listen to me, Harold,' he began, in strident tones, an admonitory finger raised, 'I just saw a huge car drawing away from your front door, containing, if these old eyes did not deceive me, that greedy capitalist Lever. You will not go far with millstones of that nature tied about your neck. We are a party of workers and peasants, remember?' 'You are right, Footy,' Harold droned, the water lapping at his chin. 'You are quite right. By their fruits ye shall know them. I want you to go forth, Footy, and say unto your children in the Labour Movement, the barefoot children in the Vales and furnaces, the workers by hand and by brain, that I shall never desert them. You speak their language. Capital will be smashed, have no doubts on that score: the City will wither away as we always said it would. I wonder if you would like a drink?' A bright gleam of happiness came into Mr Foot's eyes at this, and he graciously accepted a glass of the Meed before sweeping away to reassure the rank and file.

When he had gone Harold became most affectionate. 'There you are, Gladys,' he observed, tossing away an empty bottle to land harmlessly on the lawn, 'everybody's happy. God's in his heaven, and all is well at last. Soon we will be Texas-rich with oil. Varley tells me that by 1980 we shall have enough to supply the world several times over. Where will the Dismal Jimmies be then? Ha ha ha ha.' At this, he unfortunately made the mistake of pulling one of Mr Haines's ropes in order to sit more upright in the bath, whereupon the apparatus broke, causing the television set to shatter on the concrete floor, puncturing the tanks and releasing floods of water as the plastic roof collapsed — Harold being incapacitated by his knee.

Oh, holidays! The word itself
  Brings hope to ev'ry breast
We put our troubles on the shelf
  And have a lovely rest.

I take my suitcase from the rack
  All grim'd with winter's dust
And muse on what I need to pack
  The sun tan oil's a must.

Oh can it be that in a week
  I shall be gone from here?
Reposing in some sun-kiss'd creek
  Or strolling on the pier?

It can! But oh, alas, how short
  That sweet respite will be!
This is my melancholy thought
  As I put on the tea.

Oh dear, getting away every year is always such a commotion, and I must say that Harold has not made it easier for me with his current distaste for decision making. I went into his den in order to ascertain whether he wished me to pack his rope-soled espadrilles or the German Dr Scholl platform sandals that Herr Brandt presented him with as a memento of our visit to the Berlin Wall, only to be rudely dismissed. 'Good Heavens, Gladys!' he cried wearily from the depths of the Kumfisprung Conrantat Leatherette Corduroy Sitting Unit where he was perusing a copy of *Ajax: The Magazine for Men*. 'Can you not see that I am desperately trying to clear my desk before the Summer Recess? Pack whatever you think is necessary and be sure to tell Haines to feed the cat while we're away.'

Unhappily, Harold's private thoughts have been much disturbed in the past few days. I was just ironing the Inspector's beach togs when there came the sound of raucous shouting in Lord North Street, followed by rhythmic dancing to the captivating strains of *Zorba the Greek*, as made popular by Miss Nana Moussaka on BBC2. A moment later a flurry of blows fell

on the front door. On opening it, I found myself confronted by
a tall dignified gentleman with flared nostrils, a long black beard,
and wielding an enormous crozier. In a flash, it all came back to
me, and from the ring of grinning, unshaven faces I remembered
that it must be nice Archbishop Makarios whom I had met at
the Commonwealth Prime Ministers' Conference in the grounds
of Marlborough House in the happy days of our first
administration.

    'Dear Lady', he vouchsafed with a low bow, 'I come to
throw myself upon your husband.' 'Oh, how delightful,' I remarked, 'What an unexpected pleasure! Let me take your stick and hat.'
Refusing my assistance with a benign smile, the patriarch strode
purposefully into the house, pausing only to bestow a blessing
on his supporters in the narrow street outside. Surprising Harold,
who was catching forty winks face downwards on his desk in the
den, the man of God brought his staff down with a resounding
blow on the floor. 'Awake, awake, Father of the British People!'
he cried in fervent tones. 'Your hour has come.' 'What's that?

What's that?' enquired Harold dozily, rubbing his eyes.
'Ah, Makarios!! A face from the past! Come to do the shopping
at Marks and Spencers, no doubt. They are very good, are they
not?' 'You have got the wrong end of my stick,' cried the
Autarch of All Cyprus, fondling his beard with bejewelled fingers.
'Brigands have seized hold of my palace. Democracy as I know it
is no more. I have been made to walk along the plank. The evil
Colonels have devised this. If they are not to be checked in their
tracks, a bloody bath will engulf us all.'

In an instant, Harold leaped to his feet. 'Say no more,'
he cried, 'you can rely on us. Britain has never kowtowed to the
Fascist Hyenas of Athens. We will do everything in our power to
place you once again on your throne. Troops, Saracen Armoured
Vehicles, Hercules Aircraft, all are at your disposal. You have
only to say the word, and the vast might of our war machine will
fall upon your enemies.' Tears sprang to the eyes of the Archbishop
as he listened to Harold's impassioned harangue, and after drawing
back with arms spread wide, he swept him suddenly into a
whiskery embrace from which Harold only with great difficulty
emerged.

The exulting crowds had scarcely turned the corner when a
huge cavalcade of cars drew up to disgorge the spruce figure of
Mr Effendi, the Prime Minister of Turkey, also bent on having
Harold's ear. I was not present during their deliberations, as
Mr Haines had requested my assistance in preparing a floral
gladioli corsage for Lady Forkbender's First Night at the House
of Lords, but I assumed from Mr Effendi's happy smile and
vigorous shaking of my hand as he took his leave, that he had been
given similar assurances to those requested by the Archbishop.

As we were going to bed, I asked Harold when the British
troops would be setting out on their heroic mission to restore lib-
erty to the embattled island in the Mediterranean. 'Oh, that,'
Harold remarked in nonchalantly dismissive tones, pouring himself
a second nightcap of Bengers' Fortified Night Drink laced with
Sanatogen Rum Essence, 'these foreigners are very excitable
people. It's the sun, you know. By tomorrow they will have
forgotten all about it. Anyway, we haven't got the troops.
Old Hairy-Chops is a dead duck, I'm telling you. This Nico
Simpson is the one to watch. I will tell Callaghan to recognise him
while we're away on holiday.' And, with this, he became engrossed
in the Country Gentlemen's Wincarnis Summer Catalogue.

Oh Richard Nixon, 'tis farewell
  To thee we now must bid
Stormed at by shot and bursting shell
  Your duty still you did

What noble mind is here o'erthrown
  What monument has been toppled
The golden harvest you have sown
  By others will be reaped

Like to some ancient gothic pile
  That seemed without so safe
And yet within the beetles vile
  Did tunnel, bore and chafe

So, one bright morn, the cock'rel calls
  Hark! 'Tis a rat tat tat
The postman knocks, the building falls
  Collapsing, just like that.

Harold has been most upset ever since poor Mr Nixon
made his moving abdication speech on the television. We were on
holiday at the time in our snug second home, Lamorna in the
Scilly Isles. Harold had the Mitsubashi Colormite Miniature TV
on all night, fortifying himself with long thoughtful sips of
Phyllotone Fortifies the Over Fifties Rose Hip Drink which had
been recommended by the local doctor, Mr Trefellonym Cohen,
as a pick-me-up, and was ensconced in the old tartan chaise
longue which was left behind by the previous owners.
Within seconds of Harold turning on the apparatus, Mr Nixon's
pain-wracked visage materialised from out the ether. 'My friends,'
he exclaimed, his voice breaking with pent-up sobs, 'we have had
good times together, you and I. Yes, indeed. We have laboured
in the vineyard in the heat of the day. There have been good times,
and then again there have been bad times. But I want you all to
remember this. Theodore Roosevelt once said that every cloud
has a silver lining, and if you smile through the tears, the sun will
smile into your heart. . . ' Alas, I could hear no more, as the
air was rent on a sudden by a high wailing and scratching sound,
which at first I took to be Paddy, our labrador, wanting to be let

in, and then discovered to emanate from the chaise longue,
where Harold could be seen weeping openly with tears streaming
down his face, one hand beating at his breast, and the other
clawing at the taut canvas of the chaise.

It was some minutes before he was sufficiently recovered
to express his feelings in a coherent manner. 'Gladys,' he remarked
with solemn mien, as Mr Nixon could be seen climbing into the
Spirit of '76, smiling and waving to the Marine Band below,
'there are some moments that touch the heartstrings and awake
a sympathetic chord in every human soul. What we are witnessing
will be inscribed upon the tablets of history for all time.
The downfall of a great man, as Shakespeare said, is a tragic
business.' As if to illustrate the truth of these words, the chaise

longue chose this moment to give way, with a slow rending sound, depositing its occupant on the floor amid a tangled wreckage of rusting spars and strips of fraying tartan fabric.

The following day, our holiday idyll was interrupted by the unexpected arrival in an RAF *Waterstoat* of Mr Jim Callaghan, wearing his wellies and a wide smile, en route for the conference table at Geneva. Harold was asleep on the carpet when I ushered the beaming Foreign Secretary into the loungette-cum-breakfast bar, and showed no signs of moving at his colleague's dynamic entry. 'oh deary me, deary me,' grinned Mr Callaghan. 'I do seem to have chosen a bad time and no mistake. No, please don't bother him, I only came to tell him about the war breaking out. I can handle it though. You let him lie there. We all know he needs a good rest one way and another.'

'Callaghan,' came a quiet snarl from the still motionless figure on the carpet, where Harold had opened one eye and revealed his teeth, 'you had better watch your step. If there is any war needs declaring, I will do the declaring, thank you very much. There is still a bit of life in the old dog yet. Haines' — at this our bespectacled factotum put his peeling face through the kitchen window with an eager expression — 'bring in the *Daily Telegraph* Motorists' Map of the Far East, and Gladys, help me to my feet. I seem to have an attack of mild cramp here and there.'

Once installed on the settee in the lounge, Harold listened patiently as Mr Callaghan explained in simple terms the tragic outcome of the Cypriot troubles. 'I see it all, I see it all,' Harold concluded, lighting his pipe with slightly trembling fingers, 'this is your big moment, Jim. A figure on the international stage. You and you alone will represent Western Reason at the conference tables of the world, bringing these swarthy and excitable Levantines to heel. I leave it in your hands. You are the man of the hour. You may rely on me to back you to the hilt.' After he had gone, smiling and nodding, to be piped aboard the vertical take-off vehicle, Harold called Mr Haines in from the garden to put his shirt on and go down to The Scilly Cow. Providing him with a supply of 10p pieces, he instructed him to ring up Washington and leave a message for Mr Ford to send in Mr Kissinger at once, as things had passed beyond the point where minor politicians could be of any further use.

4th OCTOBER 1974

Once more unto the hustings ho!
The banners wave and flap
The hecklers shout their irrelevant remarks
The faithful cheer and clap

Like to Demosthenes of yore
Brave Harold wends his way
On his triumphant whistle-stop tour
No-one can him gainsay

A Lenin on the platform high
He thunders words of hope
His finger jabbing at the sky
It is not just old rope

But at the mighty leader's side
Alone, a woman sits
And ponders, wistful, moisty-eyed
Should he now call it quits?

'Tis I! A woman! Frail and mute
In times of stress a prop
Should I rise up with outstretched hand
And whisper 'Harold, stop!

'Call it a day, throw in the towel
While it is yours to throw
Assume the hood and monkish cowl
That with the Don's life go!

'And where the ancient oak-tree leans
At ease among the flowers
Master of Univ. or of Queens
Sit and write the second volume of
                        your memoirs!'

    I penned these lines in the Cardinal Wolsey Tea Bar of the Trust House Forterama Motorway Rest Lounge spanning the M631 Spur Interchange at Huxtable, Staffs, while Harold was going walkabout in the Souvenir Boutique with Mr Haines.

Though he gives every appearance of bouncing health I cannot help but reflect that the present election stress must wreak a terrible toll on Harold's constitution, especially in view of Dr Melrose's recent warning about taking things easy and cutting back on his consumption of Wincarnis and Coronario Thromboso Magnifico Grandee cigars.

The Election had been hanging over our heads for many weeks, and it was something of a relief when Harold, after a visit to Madame Gypsy Rose Baring's star-spangled booth at Battersea Funfair, plumped for October the Tenth as the day of destiny, Venus being in his cusp and Driberg in the ascendant. Mr Haines was instructed to go at once to Mr Len Murray, the gentleman who leads the toilers by hand and brain, in order to obtain his permission for the election to be held and later in the day, having gruffly given his assent, Mr Murray was good enough to drop round to Lord North Street for a schooner of Old Grand-dad Worsthorne Sparkling Perry, the Pear-Shaped Drink with the Zip.

'Well, Len,' Harold remarked as the horny-handed son of toil took a noisy sip of the Perry drink and pushed his cloth cap back on his forehead, 'you will appreciate that in the words of the late President Abraham Nixon, you cannot fool all of the people all of the time, but you can have a forkending good try, if you'll pardon my French. It is with this end in mind that Haines here at my instruction has prepared a certain document, somewhat on the lines of our well-loved Solemn and Binding Agreement drawn up between myself and your predecessor Feather in the 'sixties, which had such colossal success in stabilising the economy in those dark days. By the by,' he continued, blowing a cloud of smoke thoughtfully towards the ceiling, 'Feather has since been elevated to the Peerage, and is living now in considerable comfort, a fact which may or may not be relevant to our discussions at this moment in time. However that may be. . . Haines!' — and here he snapped his fingers to the cowering figure in the green baize apron standing by the door — 'bring in the contract and another bumper of Best Worsthorne for our guest.'

By now a ruby flush had suffused the countenance of the General Secretary, and sinking back into the settee he accepted a Thromboso de Luxe from a large deal box brought back from Cuba by Mrs Benn. 'Now,' Harold resumed, snatching a tattered sheet of typescript from the factotum's hands, 'you see here. . . Haines! I thought I told you to type this out again. It is not sufficient just to cross out "Solemn and Binding Agreement" and pencil in the words "Social Contract". Don't you realise that on this sheet of paper we stand or fall? And take that sweet out of your mouth, Foureyes, the Fate of the Nation is at stake!'

By the time the Social Contract had been retyped, Mr Murray and Harold were sitting on the floor pulling small tufts out of the carpet and laughing, and Mr Murray did little more than glance at it before drawing his pen unsteadily across the paper. He had scarcely completed this task when the Dulcitone Chimes proclaimed the arrival of Horace, Norris, Maurice, Boris and Doris McWhirter, the Incredible Quins and Proprietors of the Guinness Book of Records. 'Aha, aha!' cried Harold in welcoming strains, 'you could not have come at a better time. Mr Slurry here has just laid his Monica on the line to an historic Magna Charta, a social contract which will usher in a new era of industrial peace and prosperity. But seriously,' and here his mien grew grave, 'let me know at once what you have unearthed in pursuance of my

enquiries. Who pulled it off most times?' At this, Doris, the leader of the quins, replied in piping tones that only Mr Gladstone had managed to win four elections. There was a solemn silence, broken only by the sound of Mr Haines's

whispered curses as he tried to detach his mint from the back
of Mr Murray's woolly. Imploringly, I laid a hand on Harold's
sleeve. 'Surely,' I pleaded, 'four times! That is enough for any
man. Give me your word that if you vanquish Heath upon the
day you will hang up your spurs in the hour of triumph and
make way for nice Mr Jenkins.' 'That rat-faced traitor!' Harold
snarled, 'Why. . . ' But then, restraining himself with great effort,
he allowed a lovely smile to spread across his face. 'Of course,
Gladys, of course. Enough is enough. You have my solemn word.'

I was much reassured by this, until as I passed the Den on
my way to put Nimmo out, I heard Harold on the phone to
Lady Forkender. 'Five times, Marcia, just think of that.
One more and Gladstone's finished!' Time, I fear, for another
little word with Dr Melrose.

Hoorah! Hoorah! The cheering throng
  Salutes the conquering King
'Tis Harold! See, he strides along
  To him your tributes bring

And who is it, who cowers away
  A poor bedraggled wight,
A pallid wraith that shuns the day
  And cringes from the light?

Avaunt, be off, your day is done
  Hang up your sailor's hat
Now Mr Whitelaw should be allowed to take over
  I tell it to you flat!

I fear there may be a note of vindictiveness in these lines,
but by the end of any campaign tempers are frayed, and after
many sleepless nights in Mr Haines's Commerbus Minivan
I must admit that my nerves were in a state and this may have
coloured my view of Mr Heath in his hour of ignominy.
Harold, however, was unrepentant as he watched the late
results in the lounge of the Ethel-burga Berni Lakeland Motel
in Huyton. 'Look at him now,' he cried, quaffing deep from
a crystal flower bowl of Cyril Ray Selected Australian Spumanti
Sanilavino, and pointing derisively at the tear-stained cheek of
his erstwhile rival, captured in colour on the Bernstein Khamikaze
Portable. 'You had this coming to you Heath! Now for the death
by a thousand cuts!'

As Harold was performing his victory dance before the
television, Mr Haines cleared his throat to announce that
Mr Dimbleby had come to record a victory message to the
nation. 'At once, at once,' Harold snapped, hastily gathering up
the Italian straw-encased Magnum of sparkling health drink
and stowing it away behind the curtain. 'Show them in Haines,
and kindly pass my powder compact.'

So it was that the smiling, youthful and smartly-coiffed
communicator came confidently in to find Harold in statesman-
like pose, resting with one hand upon the television and sadly

shaking his head, as Mr Heath's rubicund features vanished down
the cathode ray tube. 'Ah, Dimbleby!' he cried. 'We have just
witnessed the tragic downfall of a great statesman. Even you,
with your brittle and superficial feelings, hardened by years
spent in the Tory media and hospitality lounge of the BBC,
must experience a pang to see this last brave effort thwarted.'

Mr Dimbleby appeared unimpressed by Harold's harangue, adjusting the shawl collar of his Mr Fish-style salt-and-pepper lurex smooching jacket and combing his eyebrows in a small pocket mirror. 'You must be feeling very pleased, Prime Minister,' he began, as the electricians assembled a ring of arc lights round the settee. 'Give me that clapper board,' insisted Harold, seizing the wooden apparatus traditionally brandished at the start of every interview, and bringing the halves together with a crack. 'Take One!!' he exclaimed. 'Mid Close-up, favouring my left profile if you would. Quiet please! Is sound running? Roll it!! No one could be more upset than I am at what must be for the Leader of the Opposition a truly shattering blow. Ted Heath was a very wonderful person, not at all the cold fish some of his detractors would have had us think. Not at all a great blubbering insensitive slob with nothing better to do than play with himself over the pianoforte. Cut! I'm sorry, David, my grief was too much for me. See to it that the final phrase is deleted. I do not want any repetition of the *Yesterday's Men* episode.'

After some adjustment of Mr Dimbleby's apparatus, the historic interview recommenced.

'Prime Minister,' Mr Dimbleby ventured. 'Putting aside for a moment your natural feelings of compassion, you must never-theless feel a sense of pride in this, your fourth victory as Prime Minister.' 'Ahem, aha,' Harold coughed discreetly, stuffing a wad of Old Mogg's Navy Twist into his Bulldog Briar, 'you know, David, this is not a time for personal rejoicing, not a time for petty party triumphs. It is with a heavy heart that we go forward from this election to confront the worst crisis this country of ours has known, certainly since 1066. God knows, I've made this point again and again, we shall need all the strength and courage and sober seriousness at our disposal if we are to survive the days of peril, of austerity and shortage that lie ahead of us. Cut! Gladys, get that drink out! Dimbleby, what is the news from Lincoln?'

Mr Dimbleby vouchsafed that nice Mr Taverne had lost his seat to the official Labour candidate. I have seldom seen Harold's face undergo a more sudden transformation. In a flash the sober countenance of the man of destiny had vanished, giving way to a gargoyle-like grimace of joy. 'Aha! That silk-tongued traitor! That softly-spoken balding Judas! Ha ha! Ha ha! One in the eye for the Cocktail Set characters at Printing House Square, I think! Back to their candle-lits soirees in NW1, the After Eight mints, their Gauloises and the Pallisers on television! The tide of history has engulfed them! Hark!' — and here he interrupted his harangue to drain the lees of the Spumanti — 'already I can hear the rumble of the tumbrils come for Smoothichops, the flash and snap of the Guillotine! All power is mine! Ha ha!'

Scarcely had Mr Dimbleby withdrawn with all his para-phernalia, than the cherubic-featured Mr Gormley was ushered in with Mr Murray to kiss hands on their appointment as Economic Overlords with special powers to imprison without trial all unproductive elements, to whit stockbrokers, speculators, Ministers of Religion, enemies of the Party, political adventurers and Woodrow Wyatt parasites.

1st NOVEMBER 1974

I do not know what has got into Harold this year, but he has suddenly taken it into his head to give a bonfire party, something he has not done since Giles has been out of short trousers. The scheme was broached over breakfast, when Harold looked up from his perusal of the *Punch* Bumper to Bumper Motorshow Number and remarked: 'Haines, I wish to invite the Leaders of all European States to a high-level Guy Fawkes Barbecue on November 5th to discuss the Crisis of the West, or something of that nature. It is time we stole some thunder from the self-styled Big Two, Giscard and Schmidt. Why, they were snivelling Parliamentary Under-Secretaries when Willi Brandt and I were laying down the foundations of Europe as we know it today. Here is the guest list, take it down and get Lady Forkender to type it out herself. It is time she did some work, after all that I have done for her: D'Estaing, G., Schmidt H., whoever is the Prime Minister of Italy when the invitations go out — the others you will find in *Whitaker*'s. I cannot recall their names, but mark this, Gladys,' he emphasised, dipping a soldier of toasted Mother's Wonderslice into his Huyton Academicals Souvenir egg-cup, 'spare no expense. A real Brock's benefit. The hot Wincarnipunch will flow like water. Confidence must be restored in sterling even if it bankrupts us all.'

Since then, his interest in the forthcoming celebration has been dampened by the onrush of events. First of all there was Mr Murray's weekly visit to present the latest list of TUC demands. 'Well, Murray,' he opined, as the TUC leader shyly entered, his suit still stained with trifle from his disastrous fact-finding night out at White's Club Soda Fountain, 'the crisis grows ever more complex and fascinating, does it not? We can think of little else. Who do you fancy yourself, Whitelaw or Sir Keith? I would be happier myself with the bumbling Cumberland squire. I would run rings round him. Imagine it' — here Harold grasped Mr Murray's demands and waved them dramatically above his head — 'he rises to his feet, like some old walrus disturbed in his subacqueous lair. He splutters, blinking sadly about him, slow and vulnerable, no match for my deft darts and dancing thrusts. Picture the scene, Len, if you will, as I clamber triumphant over the inert cadaver, the Elephant Bill *de nos jours*!!'

'Ha, ha, most apt, Prime Minister,' Mr Murray coughed
obligingly. 'Now, if you have a moment, Brother. . . '
'Ah yes, of course,' Harold resumed in businesslike tone,
'let us examine the document. Now then. No further redundancies.
That seems fairly reasonable. No-one to be sacked. Very good.
Worker representatives to replace directors should it so take their
fancy. Perfect. Government support for any firm that should go
bankrupt. Of course, of course. Yes, Murray, this is wholly in
keeping with the contract, and will present no problems I am sure.
Sir Keith, on the other hand — he is a worry is he not?
A brilliant mind, a fellow of All Souls, a cut above their present
leader. Yet, when it comes to battling on the ropes. . . Can you
see it, Murray? My left jabs in; a savage uppercut connects;
the crinkly-haired Baronet is shaken.' Harold now began to dance
about the room, throwing imaginary punches, one of which,
as bad luck would have it, struck Mr Haines on the bridge of the
nose as he entered noiselessly with the *Financial Times* report.
Harold was most apologetic, but Mr Haines, searching about the
carpet for the fragments of his shattered spectacles, said it was of
no consequence and that he had only come in to announce that
there had been a further tumble on the money market, and the
whole of Scotland was entirely strikebound.

It was later in the day when a series of loud explosions from
Harold's den filled me with alarm lest the dreaded Red Hand had
struck again at the soft under-belly of the Establishment.
But a whizzing rocket, scattering after it a shower of golden rain,
revealed that it was only the Inspector carrying out a routine test.

O winter trees! Now nude and bare
You raise your arms aloft;
An old man on an iron chair —
He has a nasty cough.

Bleak is the sky, the leaves whirl down
The wind moans dark and chill.
There is no joy in this grim town
Life is a bitter pill.

On pavements stacked with plastic bags
The rotting refuse lies.
The dustmen, now, we learn, old lags
Avert their shifty eyes.

Worse is to come, the polar wind,
The ice age creeping back;
Despair engulfs each lonely mind
The outlook is decidedly black.

Harold has been in a brown study all week following the unsuccessful Euro-bang Guy Fawkes spectacular in the garden, to which he had invited the heads of state of several European countries. Alas, none of them felt able to accept the invitation owing to last-minute prior commitments, so that we were left with only Mr Haines, Mr Driberg and his foreign friend at present working as a waiter, Mrs Short and Manny Shinwell's grandson, who is just retiring, to burn a rather damp effigy of Mr Taverne made of old cushions and dressed in one of Mr Benn's cast-off dinner jackets and a deer-stalker hat sent round by Mrs Jenkins.

Harold's mood has not been lightened by the mysterious affair of the missing papers. We first suspected that something was wrong when Mr Lever came round to fill in Harold's tax returns. As the twinkling gnome of Manchester was unscrewing his gold-nibbed pen prior to drawing up a list of business expenses incurred in the financial year '73 to '74, Mr Haines was sorting through the piles of restaurant bills, moving the decimal point wherever appropriate. 'Now then,' beamed the Mancunian master-mind, 'what about suits? Naturally, wearing smart clothes

is a vital part of your work, is it not, eh, ha ha, ho ho?'
'No,' Harold riposted, drawing on his pipe, 'I always wear the
same one. My father gave it to me on his deathbed. They knew
how to make suits in those days.' Mr Lever removed his spectacles
and cleaned them pensively. 'Nevertheless, there is the upkeep,
pressing and general valeting, eh? Shall we say two thou?'
'No,' replied Harold sagely, 'any spongeing, pressing, wiping off
stains and sewing on of buttons, that is all performed by Haines,
and I may say that over the years his skills in that department
have become considerable.' At this, Mr Haines, who had moved
on to polishing the EPNS on his green baize pinny in a corner of
the room, beamed gratefully and fluttered his eyelashes.

'Aha,' cried Mr Lever, 'I think we see an opening here.
Haines is your factotum. Inside staff. I think he is allowable.
And you must have someone else to help you with your secretarial
work, do you not?' At this Harold became agitated. 'Now Lever,'
he growled, grasping the diminutive entrepreneur by the lapels,
'you had better watch your lip. What concern is it of yours who
takes down my correspondence?' 'Please, please,' soothed the
latter-day Keynes with upraised hands, 'do not misunderstand me.
I am simply trying to explore whatever avenues might lead to
some advantage in the presentation of your fiscal structure.'
'Well,' said Harold grudgingly, 'that side of things is taken care
of by supporters of our cause, both here and overseas, who would
of course prefer a certain anonymity.' 'Quite so, quite so,
I understand that perfectly. But surely there are stubs, invoices,
receipts? All this would help you to reduce your taxable income,
if you follow me.' 'I regret to say,' Harold remarked after a wild
look at the ceiling, 'that all such documentation has mysteriously
vanished. Some months ago. A burglary. A break-in. Yes, that was
it. Haines, you recall it, do you not?' Mr Haines peered up
helpfully, moving his mint from one cheek to another.

'Of course you do,' Harold resumed. 'The broken glass,
the trail of blood, the papers blowing from the safe in the
midnight breeze.' Mr Lever scratched thoughtfully at his right
cheek with his index finger. 'I see,' he observed at length.
'That is most unfortunate, as in the absence of any documentary
evidence relating to these philanthropic gifts, we shall be unable
to declare them to the Revenue.' 'I agree,' Harold concurred,
'it is most unfortunate, but there we are. Now that you have
raised the matter, I will draw Trimfittering's attention to the
theft. At the time I thought it of little importance, I must confess.
One burglar more or less in Lord North Street. Alas, it is all too

common nowadays. The crime figures have increased alarmingly. Bob Mark was saying so only the other day.'

Later that same evening, I laid aside my copy of the *Lord Longford Book of Records* to pop downstairs and give the plants a drink, something I had neglected to do earlier. Imagine my surprise, walking soft-footed in my Barbara Cartland Thistledown Slipslops, to find Harold in the kitchen, bent over the waste-disposal unit, into which he was feeding sheaves of soggy paper, thrusting them into the grinding device with the handle of my wooden spoon. 'Aha, Gladys!' he cried brightly as he became aware of my presence, 'Haines has foolishly stopped up the drain with wrappings from his Colonel Sterling's finger-licking chicken. Go to bed now, I have the matter in hand.'

Oh dear Sir John, my humble thanks
For your new slender book
I like the old-fashioned looking print
I read it while I cook

'A Nip in the Air' it's called, most apt
At this autumnal tide
For we are neither of us getting any younger
As into old age we slide

But ah, how touching that you should
Include in this fair screed
Your lines about our trip to Diss!
Yes, it was bliss indeed!

A nip not only in the air
Will keep that mem'ry bright
A nip too from your silver flask
When we stopped to have a bite

Nip, nip away, grey-haired old bard
Tap at your Olivetti
Just think of all the joy you bring
To folk like my Auntie Betty.

Imagine my delight, after the Inspector had gone through
the post for bombs, to unwrap a parcel in pink tissue paper from
Hatchard's bookshop in Piccadilly, containing Sir John Betjeman's
new collection of poems, *A Nasty Nip in the Air*, with a hand-
written inscription in purple ink, *'To my dear friend Gladys,
in memory of many happy hours spent in each other's company
down at the boozer'.* Harold snatched it up in a temper when
he saw it, crying, 'What is this, Gladys? What have you been up
to now behind my back? A nip in the air, eh? A nip in the behind,
more likely, if I know these literary folk.' 'Come now,' I riposted
— as I will not hear a word said against Sir John — 'You are being
unkind. The Poet Laureate and I are literary friends, linked by
the common bond of poesy.' 'Ha ha ha ha,' Harold chuckled
cruelly, 'what about that, Haines? Eh?' At this, he dug Mr Haines
sharply in the ribs with his elbow. 'Have you considered, Gladys,

my standing with the electorate? A buffoon, a silly husband, who earns his money at the office while his wife goes train-spotting with some high-falutin' arty type. There are no flies on that kind of person, I can tell you.' At this the Inspector muttered something about his boots being on the wrong feet, and Harold said no more, tossing the slim volume on the breakfast table, and taking up the *Socialist Worker* to retire to the toilet.

This has not been an easy week at Lord North Street. Trying to get my Christmas list sorted out, I have time and time again been interrupted by affairs of state. On Thursday evening I was going through the Littlewoods Bumper Xmas Catalogue, looking for some novelty for Giles, when the sound of raucous shouting in the street outside made me draw back the curtain and peep out.

I espied the figure of Mr Gormley on our doorstep, being held up by the collar by a number of rough men, who seemed to be somewhat the worse for wear. 'I can't, boys, I can't!' Mr Gormley was protesting as his companions jostled him towards the threshold. Immediately the biggest of the men took Mr Gormley's head in his hands and hammered it three times very loudly against the door, remarking, 'Gang in theya, you daft booger, or we'll hae your guts frae fooking garters' or something of the sort. By now Harold had come out of the Den to see what was afoot, and the Inspector wrenched open the front door with his burglar's friend at the ready. Mr Gormley stood alone on the doorstep, cross-eyed and swaying slightly, his curly lock of hair rumpled in the fracas, as the sound of running feet died away down the quiet street.

'Well, Gormley?' Harold enquired, removing his pipe. 'What is all this about?' 'Please, Sir,' quavered the miners' leader, 'the lads, that is my colleagues on the Executive, er, we, that is they. . . ' 'Come to the point, come to the point,' snapped Harold. At this Mr Gormley drew his breath in sharply, puffed out his cheeks and vouchsafed: 'I am instructed by my Executive to give warning that failing the immediate award of a one hundred pound across the board increase in basic rates of pay it is our intention to call an immediate strike resulting in a total breakdown of the economy. Goodnight.' With this, Mr Gormley spun round on the spot and took a few self-confident steps along the pavement before breaking into a sprint, shouting as he did so, 'Lads! Lads! Wait for me! I did it!'

Harold was plainly incensed by what had occurred, and immediately summoned Mr Foot from his desk in the British Museum Reading Room. It was not long before the silver-haired bibliophile was ensconced in our settee, a copy of *Cobbett on Turnpikes* protruding from his capacious waistcoat pocket,

and his gnarled fingers cradling a glass of hot Marks and Spencers Yuligrog. 'Now listen to me, Footy,' Harold rasped, pacing angrily up and down, 'I have just had Gormley in here, and he made certain outrageous demands, quite at variance with the letter and spirit of your contract that you made me sign some months ago. What are you going to do about it?' Mr Foot drummed his fingers on his glass and stared into the Electric Kosiglo in pensive mood. 'Well?' prompted Harold. 'Where is your contract now?'

'Prime Minister,' began the sage, 'when you and I were boys, we had a dream...' 'Shut up!' Harold snapped. 'Where will it end, that's what I want to know. The way it's going, these miners will soon be getting more than we do. Have you thought of that?' 'I have,' replied Mr Foot in measured tones, his old eyes flashing in the firelight, 'and I see nothing intrinsically wrong in that.' 'Out!' roared Harold. 'When I brought you into the Cabinet it was on the understanding that you would pull your bloody horns

on the loonie end of things. You should be out at the pithead
now, weaving a spell of oratory over these overpaid, misguided
people. I am fed up with it, do you hear? I do dirty work as well,
and I accept a reasonable wage.'

Harold, who had been pacing vigorously, waving his pipe
to emphasise his points, suddenly paused, and stood on tiptoe
to adjust one of the Peter Scott flight of china ducks that was
hanging slightly crooked. 'Alright,' he continued at length in
a calmer tone, 'pay him this time. But I warn you Foot,
next time I shall be extremely cross.'

Harold has suddenly become interested in the Common Market again, and it has been just like the old days with General de Gaulle when he and George Brown made a triumphant progress through the cultural centres of our European Heritage with such unfortunate results. But now, as I heard Harold remarking to Mr Haines while the latter was kneeling to brush the fluff out of his turnups, the days of the Grand Seigneur are gone for ever, and today we see new men at the helm, the technocrats, the administrators. It was in this spirit that we set off on *HMS Richard Marsh III* Hoverspeed Craft from Dover, in response to a delightful embossed invitation from Monsieur Giscard to take part in a fact-finding entertainment in Paris at the Crazy Horse Saloon.

Harold had been most anxious to pop over to the French capital for many weeks, but every time he rang up to arrange a date the President was unobtainable owing to unspecified pressures. 'You mark my words,' said the Inspector, with a raucous chuckle. 'I know these Frogs. Can't get enough of it.' 'Be quiet,' Harold had rasped, 'when I require your guttersnipe observations I will ask for them. No, the President is a man of the people. I am told that at night he roams the streets incognito, seeing for himself what problems French men and women have to wrestle with.'

So it was that we arrived at Boulogne, in the company of Sailor Jim Callaghan, looking a trifle queasy at the gills.

'Now then, Callaghan,' Harold observed as the *Orange Arrow* Minitrain sped through the vineyards and tin huts of Normandy, 'there will be no giving way. Our position is clear. Either they accept our terms or we get out.' 'Oho,' Mr Callaghan chuckled, taking a swig from his duty-free half-litre Glen Tooley 90% Proof Liqueur Chocolate Santakeg. 'Very amusing. Most droll. Pull the other.' 'Callaghan!' Harold snapped impatiently. 'Just you remember this. I was Prime Minister of England when Schmidt was an errand boy at *Punch* and Giscard was cleaning out the ash-trays at the Banque Natouest de Paris. It is as the senior statesman that I come. You will not find me being pushed about by these new boys.'

On our arrival on foot at the Elysee Palace we were somewhat taken aback to find the windows shuttered and a large notice outside in French saying it was for sale through Knight Frank and Rutley Ltd. 'There must be some mistake,' Harold vouchsafed, dropping his tartan grip on the doorstep and pulling at the rusted bell. 'This is the President's Official Residence. I have been here several times, Jim, when de Gaulle was alive. It is all in my memoirs. That fountain over there is where George Brown. . . ' At this moment the door creaked open to reveal a frail old lady, bent and gnarled, smoking a cigarette. 'Aha, Madame,' Harold began in his fluent French: 'Excusez-moi, mais we are looking for le President.' 'Parti, parti,' quavered the crone with a gesture of dismissal. 'No, no,' Jim interposed, 'not a party. Monsieur le President.'

At length the old lady summoned her husband, a moustached veteran in a black beret smoking a clay pipe, who told us a most interesting anecdote about how he lost his arm at the battle of Verdun. Eventually, he directed us to the President's private penthouse flat in a fashionable district of the city. Unfortunately Monsieur Giscard was out when we arrived, and his receptionist, an elegantly dressed young lady wearing the latest Autumn fashions, invited us to sit in some low modern leather bags of sawdust while she made certain enquiries. Before she was able to do so, however, a telephone warbled, and the receptionist was engaged for some minutes by a shrill female voice, who the young lady addressed as Madame from time to time, shrugging her shoulders and shaking her head. From what I could understand the demure receptionist was explaining that the President had gone out for a few hours for a meeting with a Mr Wolfson and a Mr Coolihands from Angleterre. The caller, however, did not seem disposed to believe this information, and rang off in a rage. Some time later a well-endowed lady in a fur coat, filling the room with a heavy aroma of expensive scent, strode in and deposited a heap of jewelry on the desk, saying that the President could perhaps do something with it. She was followed at intervals by a young woman in tears wearing a shawl and carrying a baby, an irate gentleman with a poker in his hand, and a page-boy from a hotel carrying a large purple envelope smudged with red lipstick.

At eight o'clock Harold said he had had enough and was in a sulk. At Jim's suggestion therefore we adjourned to a colourful old-world cafe called *Les Deux Fagots* with tables on the

pavement heated by overhead Kosiglo fires. After a few glasses
of a delightful aniseed drink mixed with water, Harold became
convivial, and was recounting tales of the old days with George,
when suddenly we espied the lean, balding figure of Monsieur
Giscard ambling happily along the street dressed in patent
leather thigh boots, angora riding breeches and a black suede
studded Rocker's Coat. On either arm he embraced a young
lady, one of them from Africa, and one apparently from the
Orient, both of whom I took from his attentiveness to be
visiting diplomats. On seeing him, Harold sprang up with a cry,

and after an altercation with the waiter, at the end of which we were obliged to pay a bill for thirty-five pounds including TAV, we ran along the pavement through the bustling crowds of Christmas shoppers.

'Monsieur, monsieur,' Harold called, as we drew level with the President, 'c'est moi, Mr Wilson.' 'Oh, mon dieu!' Monsieur Giscard exclaimed. 'Excusez-moi, my darlings, I must talk with this little man for just one tiny moment.' Despite the President's enchanting French smile, his companions pouted sulkily and looked about them. 'As you see, Tommy,' the President continued with a charming twitch of the eyebrows, 'I have rather a lot on my hands. Why don't you give my secretary a buzz when you get back to London?' With this he blew me a most delightful kiss, nodded dismissively to Harold and Jim, and turning on his heel, vanished once more into the Parisian throng. Since then, Harold has been very bad-tempered, and even Jim Callaghan singing sea-shanties on the Hovercraft coming back failed to lift his gloomy spirits.

10th JANUARY 1975

O welcome 1975
  Farewell the dying year;
Here's hoping this our land will thrive
  Come, lads, and raise a cheer!

Though economic crisis looms
  And nasty bombs go off
Though upward the inflation zooms
  Affecting tramp and toff

Must we be therefore down at heart?
  Must we despair and sulk?
No, no! Let each one play his part
  To salvage this old hulk

Hope springs eternal, it is said
  'Tis dark before the dawn
'Tis darker when we rise from bed
  On January morn

Outside the cold may be intense
  Jack Frost obscures the pane
Within we gladly count our pence
  And try not to complain

A kindly heart is oft
  · More dear than worldly gain
And one old lady's smile so soft
  Worth any sheik's domain.

Imagine our surprise, on the morning after our return from
a brief and somewhat bleak British Rail Away-Break Middle of
the Week Winter Excursion All Inclusive Tour of Manchester
where we spent a quiet Christmas, to hear a wailing voice
emanating from the tower of St John's, Smith Square, calling
the Faithful to Prayer. At the same moment, the sound of soft
Silver Phantom Rolls Royces drawing up outside the house sent
Mr Haines scurrying to take his hair out of curlers and open the
front door. There stood Mr Healey, dressed in a soup-stained
ankle-length overcoat with a tea towel tied round his head,

accompanied by a multitude of small friends, all bearded and with twinkling black eyes flashing from under their Old Testament style burnouses. 'Ah, Prime Minister,' exclaimed Mr Healey as Harold and I came forward to greet our unexpected guests, 'Your Sublime Highness, Sheik Yamani Oryalife, allow me to present our managing director, Harold Pasha.'

Harold appeared somewhat nonplussed as the men of the East inclined their heads, and taking the initiative I cried, 'Come in, come in, and let me take your towelling.'
Soon the ground floor of Lord North Street was filled with the aromatic smoke of bubbling hookah pipes, while Haines and the Inspector were busy arranging cushions on the floor in obedience to our new friends' silent gestures. Fortunately, my Aunt Betty had given us a box of crystallised grapefruit segments from W.H. Smith for Christmas, which I was able to pass round the host of seated potentates, and the Inspector obliged by pouring out from a good strong pot of Lyons' Instiblend Goolagong. 'Now,' said Mr Healey at length, lowering himself into Giles's inflatable Whoopee Cushion, 'let us get down to brass tacks. Harold, these gentlemen have a very interesting proposition to make which I believe could make a substantial difference to our economic situation.'

'Well, I think I should make it quite clear at the outset,'
began Harold, puffing at his pipe, 'that we are not beggars.
There has been a flood of loose talk, particularly in the Tory
press, about so-called collapses of the system and so forth.
Nothing of the kind has occurred. As you see' — here he waved
a hand at the Kosiglo fire — 'all public services are functioning
normally. We are not interested in charity. What I am sure my
colleague is talking about is a medium-term loan of say
five hundred billion dollars, interest-free, to be paid back at the
end of some reasonable period, let us say for the sake of argument,
a hundred years.' 'Now, now, Harold,' Mr Healey soothed.
'That is not what these gentlemen are offering. What is proposed,
Prime Minister, is that our friends should make us a reasonable
cash offer for the British Isles, to be obtained by a compulsory
purchase order. I think on the face of it that this is a very
attractive proposition.'

Mr Healey looked around the circle of bearded sheiks,
who nodded and smiled. Anticipating any possible reservations
on Harold's part, the Chancellor continued, 'You may rest
assured that your own position, at least as far as the appearances
are concerned, will remain unchanged, and in perpetuity following
the abolition of elections.' At this Harold's face brightened.
'Now gentlemen', Mr Healey continued, 'are there any further
points to be cleared up?' There was silence for a moment,
and much benign shaking of heads, but then, to my surprise,
one wizened Emir delved deep into his flowing robes and
extracted a tattered press cutting which he proceeded carefully
to unfold. As he passed it around for our perusal, I saw that it
was a photograph of Harold being clasped to the ample bosom
of Mrs Golda Meir, while tears streamed down her face.
'This not good,' remarked our oriental guest succinctly.
'This very naughty. We not like.' All his companions craned
over to see, and nodded vigorously, expressing marked distaste
for Mrs Meir's figure and personal attributes. 'Bad vibes, man,'
observed another Elder. 'Golda bad chick. No more of this,
we pray.' Harold seemed irrationally annoyed and, snatching
the photograph from the gnarled hands of a Bedouin who
was examining it upside down with clucks of disapproval,
he tore it to shreds.

'Healey!' he shouted. 'This is insufferable. My private life
is my own affair. It is no business of the gutter press with whom
I choose to spend my leisure hours.' 'Bad woman, bad woman,'
muttered the Elder obdurately. 'And you belt up, Goat Features!'

Harold snapped, at which a growing hubbub of outrage filled the room, and it was not long before our visitors were elbowing their way towards the door, ignoring the despairing pleas of Mr Healey to consider a reduced offer.

'Well, that's torn it,' the Chancellor vouchsafed as the last Rolls Royce purred from the kerb. 'Bang goes your chance of staying on top for 20 years. I'm afraid it will have to be Callaghan and a National Government.' 'Oh, come on, Denis!' Harold cried defiantly, slapping Mr Healey on the back and leading him into the Den for a Wincarnigrog and Twiglets. 'You are wasting your time with these camel-dung wallahs. Just wait till I have sorted Schmidt and Giscard out, and when the oil is flowing the Market will soon look up. We will sell, but when the time is right. Which reminds me, Haines, be sure to cash in my Post Office Savings Bonds, will you, before they become entirely worthless. I want to buy some socks from Marks and Spencers.'

From Erin's green island
 Where leprechauns stalk
I come back to my land
 By Tourist from Cork

Farewell bonny Ireland
 Now part of the Nine
Europa's green bulwark
 The Treaty doth sign

Flow softly, sweet Liffey
 Through Dublin's grey town
Where Irishmen squiffy
 Their Guinnesses down

  (Chorus)

O Harold must you leave?
 O Harold must you go?
But sure, 'tis not the final bow
 Leastways, we hope not so.

  I penned these lines after enjoying a delicious glass of
Old Paddy's Gaelic Cocoa during our two-day Away From It All
Sealink Winterbreak at the Royal Waldorf Shamrock Hotel,
just opposite Dublin Airport's Number One Runway.
I must say that for what promised to be a dramatic eyeball-to-
eyeball Walk with Destiny, Harold was remarkably relaxed as
we set off with Jim Callaghan in the Aer Lingus Motorcoach
from the Kensington Terminal.

  Jim seemed most convivial, fortifying himself from time
to time from a stone bottle of some foreign drink sent to him by
an admirer in Germany and laughing outrageously as Harold
outlined the many obstacles that lay in our path, seemingly
insurmountable: New Zealand butter, our contribution to
the Budget, and a host of allied traps. 'You see, Gladys,'
said Harold, 'it is like the Horse of the Year Show. The five-bar
gate,' ('Ho ho ho' from Jim), 'the wall,' ('Ha ha ha'), 'the water-
jump' — at this Mr Callaghan did the nose trick, and had to be

slapped on the back by an obliging Irish steward — 'I cannot think that in all my long experience I have had to face a tougher assignment. The odds are astronomical. Only a superman could come through.'

Mr Callaghan continued to splutter into his handkerchief, particularly when Mr Haines appeared with a stack of roneoed scripts which Harold hastily tucked away in his Aer Lingus Bag, but not before I had had a chance to glimpse the words 'Final Communique: It's Yes Says Wilson: Spectacular Triumph for British PM says Top Eurobrass'. I did not understand the significance of this, especially as the Conference had yet to take place, but Mr Haines has always moved in a mysterious way, as Lady Forkender observed.

On arrival at the Immigration Disinfectant Sheep-Dip, a precaution against IRA Terrorists and Foot and Mouth Disease, Jim had his wellington boots confiscated for the duration of our stay, while Harold posed grim-faced for photographers, telling reporters that it was touch and go and that there was hard bargaining ahead. We then drove by taxi to the hotel. Harold approached the emerald-uniformed receptionist to ask if there were any messages. 'What name would it be, Sorr?' the latter enquired in a thick brogue and, on hearing who it was, replied that there were six foreign gentlemen waiting to see him in the W.B. Yeats Annexe on the third floor.

Imagine my surprise on entering the tastefully appointed lounge, to find the Heads of the six Common Market countries sitting in their shirtsleeves in a dishevelled state, watching the colour television, on which a group of middle-aged ladies in green kilts were jumping up and down to the sound of raucous fiddling.

'Ach so, Harold,' remarked Herr Schmidt, removing a cigar from his mouth, 'so you are here at last already. For the folk's sake let's pull our thumbs out and get on with it.' 'Quite so, quite so, all in good time,' remarked Harold brightly, peeling his jacket off and indicating to Haines that he should lock the door. The languid form of Monsieur Giscard could be descried stretched out on a tweed-covered Put-U-Up by the window as he murmured reassuring Gallic noises into the telephone to someone called Cherry. As we drew near he looked up, and consulted his watch. 'Enfin,' he observed, 'il est arrive, le petit con,' — a slang term which I took to express affectionate regard.

'Now then, gentlemen,' Harold began. 'You know of course that there is no question of our pulling out. All I ask in return is a group photograph and your silence at the final press conference. I also think it would give a little polish to proceedings were we to provide the media with one exhausting late-night session.' At this there was a grumble of protest, led by Monsieur Giscard. 'Do not misunderstand me, please,' Harold went on. 'There will be no necessity for any actual negotiation. Jim has brought the dice and playing cards, and I have asked the management to arrange for video cassette equipment to be installed with a selection of old films. What is essential is that the lights should be seen to be blazing until at least one thirty while we appear to grapple with these momentous issues.'

I myself took the afternoon off to visit the Eamonn Andrews Museum at his birthplace in Cosgrave Street, and to buy a knitted Arran island hat for the Inspector. When I returned that evening, I found hordes of cameramen surrounding good-looking Mr Wheeler from the BBC, who was just explaining for the viewers at home that the negotiations had now reached a crucial stage, that Harold had threatened to walk out, and that British membership hung by a thread. 'The situation here is desperately tense,' he concluded with serious mien.

Inside the W.B. Yeats Annexe the scene was not a pleasant one. On the conference table, Herr Schmidt was giving a demonstration of Bavarian dancing, and Monsieur Giscard was looking most depressed, leafing through the pages of a coloured magazine. Harold and Mr Haines were sitting in front of the closed circuit television, watching *The Dam Busters* and occasionally cheering, while other delegates played darts or slept. I tiptoed out the back way, where I had come in, reflecting upon the mystery of it all.

The following morning, before the massed reporters, Harold at last, unshaven and heavy-eyed, informed us that, following prolonged negotiations, his colleagues had agreed to give way in all important areas and accept defeat. Mr Haines did his best to start an ovation, but without success.

> *Hail, Primavera! See her come*
> *With Mother Nature's gown*
> *The green buds break, the bees all hum*
> *The blossom flutters down*
>
> *Hail, swallow! Welcome returnee*
> *From Afric's warmer clime*
> *How thrilled each little bird must be*
> *To come here at this time*
>
> *See! Fur and Feather doth embrace*
> *To procreate their kind*
> *A smile lurks on the pigeon's face;*
> *Her beau doth strut behind*
>
> *Why, midst this jocund Rite of Spring*
> *Should my own spirits flag?*
> *O tell me, Cuckoo, carolling*
> *Why is life such a drag?*

I have tried to express in these poor lines my own sense of disquiet during the last few days. Try as I may, I cannot but feel that the future holds little but an uphill struggle with mounting difficulties. Could it be that we shall one day look back on 1975 as the 'good old days' when Len Murray and Mr Benn laid the foundations for a Socialist Britain?

Perhaps it is only the poet in me, as Sir John has often intimated, that is in touch, through the delicate antennae of artistic sensibility, with the deeper vibrations of the Universe. I was ironing the Inspector's long combs before storing them away with their moth-balls in the upstairs airing cupboard, when Mr Healey tapped on the kitchen window, making signals that he wished to enter. Enjoying a cup of Nestea and a Disneyland Cookie in the dining area prior to Harold's return from the Vauxhall Road Working Men's Club Billiard Rooms, where he has taken to going with Mr Haines in the afternoons, Denis admitted that he was worried lest, as he put it, we might be overtaken by events.

I did not quite understand what he meant until, when Harold returned full of bonhomie and smoking a cigar, it all came pouring out. For too long, Denis said, they had pinned their faith in Mr Murray and his friends in the hope that they would play ball and bring home the bacon. And what had happened? They were now up ship creek and had lost their paddle. It was all very well Mr Foot going on about the Tolpuddle Martyrs, but that was a long time ago, and things had changed since then. Somewhere somebody was going to have to take a stand, and the Railwaymen were next in line.

Harold seemed rather inattentive as Mr Healey spluttered on. He had helped himself to a balloon glass of Kagan Export Five-Star Vodka, left behind as a memento by Mr Shelepin, and was now holding it up in the sunlight, making a little Fairy Tinkerbell effect on the flowered wallpaper.
'An old fashioned run on the pound', continued Mr Healey, 'cannot be ruled out. If it should come, we are done for.'
For some time there was silence, save for the sound of Mr Healey eating biscuits. Then Harold, tiring of the rainbow pattern on the wall, emptied his glass and observed:
'Denis, did you see Mike Yarwood on Saturday? I thought he did you very well. He caught that curious toothy, furry little look you've got. Did you think it amusing? Gladys and I had a good chuckle, didn't we dear?' I must confess that I had not seen the programme that Harold was referring to, but thought it best to nod and smile.

Mr Healey was about to empty his mouth of biscuits and reply, when the door flew open and in popped the wide-eyed Mr Benn, his pipe projecting at a breezy angle from his clenched teeth. 'Well', Harold enquired sleepily, 'what have you done now, Barmy?' Mr Benn ignored the soubriquet, and whisked a folder from his briefcase. 'Here it is,' he proclaimed. 'Sir Don's bomb-shell report on British Leyland. Your friend Lord Stokes is to be put on trial before the People's Tribunal. He will confess to errors of bourgeois deviationism.' 'Very amusing, Tony,' Harold observed. 'It will make a good turn at the Keep Britain Out Gala Dance and Social you and Vanessa Redgrave are putting on at the Roundhouse next week. But tell us, Benn, as a matter of interest — Denis here has been rabbiting on, haven't you Denis, about these wage claims and so forth — how would you deal with the crisis on the Railways, if you were PM or, as you would put it, Chairman of the Central Committee? The men are asking for 30% and there is no money left in the kitty.'

With this Harold sat down, folded his arms and looked
Mr Benn rather blearily in the eye. The latter, however, did not
pause before replying: 'I suggest the Government immediately
takes over British Rail, making it a state-owned corporation.
It is as easy as that. That is the Socialist answer.'

Mr Healey stood up, emptied the remainder of the vodka
into his mug and, with a trembling hand, raised it to his lips.
Harold nodded for some minutes. 'Well, Tony,' he said at last,
'there is a lot in what you say. My cottage in the Scilly Isles
is standing empty at the moment. Why not go down there and
work this out in detail? Take time over it. A month, two
months, three months. . . A State-owned railway system. Yes,

I like it more and more. And now, if you will excuse us, Haines and I have got to work out where the Ballot Boxes are to be delivered for the Referendum. Will it be Earl's Court, will it be the Albert Hall, or perhaps an entirely new, surprise location in the Vauxhall Road to get round the security? Gentlemen, I must leave you, there are important issues to be decided.'

Mr. Benn was the first to start up from the reverie that followed Harold's words. 'Fine!' he cried, snapping shut his briefcase. 'Super!' — and with this he stepped sharply out into the garden and hopped away across the lawn. Harold and Mr Haines then left, taking their cues from the rack in the hall. Mr Healey rose slowly to his feet, and began to bang his head against the wall. . .

Oh Chelsea, famed for bud and bloom
*　For pensioners and buns*
Where now the fragrant roses loom
*　Athwart the rusting guns.*

Mecca of all green-fingered folk
*　In this last week of May*
Where sweet old ladies pry and poke
*　Beneath the blossoms gay.*

O could we but for ever rove
*　Within thy fragrant tents*
And savour Nature's treasure trove
*　Regardless of expense!*

I have always loved the Chelsea Flower Show, so imagine my pleasure when Harold accepted a delightful gold-embossed invitation to join Sir Monty and Lady Fison in the CBI Dig for Victory Tent on the opening day. I was particularly delighted when Sir John Betjeman immediately agreed to escort me, as I knew that Harold would be tied up talking shop with Sir Monty and his colleagues. So we set off, on a lovely May morning, with Mr Haines at the wheel of his Mini, and myself, Harold and Lady Forkbender in the back. There was Sir John, waiting for us on the doorstep of his bijou artisan's cottage in Chelsea, a delightful lady passer-by brushing the collar of his coat and adjusting his floppy hat.

'Gosh, isn't this fun?' he panted as he clambered in to join us in the back of the vehicle, coming to rest, somewhat cautiously, on Harold's lap. Luckily we had not far to go, as I could see Harold was not wholly at ease trying to smoke his pipe with Britain's Premier Poet perched incongruously on top of him. Once through the wrought-iron gates, with the glorious scent of the flowers and the music of a military band drifting through the trees, we were in another world. Harold has never been particularly interested in flowers, and he and Mr Haines and Lady Forkbender made a beeline for the CBI Tent, where Harold said he was sure they would be able to obtain a cool drink.

It is hard for me, even now, when I have rubbed shoulders with potentates and astronauts, to realise my good fortune in walking side by side with Sir John through massed banks of carnations. With his dignified gait and silver-topped walking stick, doffing his panama right and left to the many people who recognised him from his performances on TV, he cut a

distinguished figure, and I was delighted by his observations about the teeming life on every side. 'Gosh, Gladys,' he whispered, 'do look at the old lady in gloves. I bet she's come up for the day on the 8.40 stopping train from Stroud. Mrs Sniggs, the Vicar's wife, glad to get away from the old boy for a bit. Lunch at Barker's and then back on the 4.15.'

What a privilege to be vouchsafed this glimpse into the workings of the creative mind! Alas, a glimpse was all it was to be, for at that moment Mr Haines came running up to say that Lady Fison was most anxious we should join her for a glass of pink champagne, an invitation which Sir John very readily accepted.

In the tent, which was decorated with pennants advertising fertiliser, a lavish exhibition of different sorts of drink had been set out on a table, and Harold and Mr Haines were tasting some new varieties of Polish vodka with pieces of grass in them. Sir John gravitated towards a small 'Pool Environment' which had been created in one corner to advertise pond detergents, where he sat in a striped folding chair, sipping the pink beverage and looking from the brightly-painted little Fisognomes labouring by the pool to the pattern of leaves shadowing the roof of the marquee.

After toasts had been drunk, Sir Monty, a stout, rather florid gentleman in a charcoal suit with a rose pinned to his buttonhole, cleared his throat and made a short speech, in which he extended a warm welcome to Harold, while at the same time expressing fears about the very severe disasters at present befalling British Industry. At this Harold began to laugh and, rising to his feet, exclaimed in genial tones, 'Gentlemen, I think you all know Monty doesn't need to mince words with me. Speaking off the record, and I know there are no bugs on the flowers, thanks to your excellent products' — at this there was loud laughter and applause from the assembled Captains of Industry, causing Harold to raise his hand — 'that bloody fool Benn will not be worrying you for much longer, I can assure you. I have only to get this little business of the Referendum out of the way, and then I will be packing him off to Northern Ireland. There is a time for pruning, and on June 6th it's out with the secateurs. Snip! Snip! And he will be gone! You have my solemn word.'

Later in the day a Rolls Royce purred to a halt outside the front door of Lord North Street, and an agitated Caroline Benn forced her way into the house, waving a bejewelled umbrella at Mr Haines and coming straight through to the kitchen, where Harold was sitting in his shirt sleeves enjoying a tumbler of Old Pimms and reading the football results. 'Harold, my dear,' she rasped in her attractive New England drawl, 'I know this can't be true, but Brenda Fison has been

onto me for just hours and she is very, very confused.
Tony is in tears. It's too incredible.' 'Calm yourself, my dear
Mrs Benn,' Harold soothed from his low chair. 'A mere form
of words. These big-time hotshots have to have a bit of jam
spread on it some of the time. There's not a word of truth in it,
obviously. I cannot conceive of a Cabinet without Tony.
His job is a hundred per cent secure. You can tell him that
from me.'

Eventually calmed, Mrs Benn departed in a flurry of torn-
up parking tickets, and Lady Forkbender came round to play
Canasta.

A massive 'Yes'! The people speak
 In answer to the quiz
Now from the 'No's' we hear no squeak
 A triumph sure it is

O Wedgwood Benn, where is thy sting?
 O Foot thy victory?
Thou Peter Shore hast had thy fling
 And so hath Len Murree

So into Europe proud we go
 With Harold at our head
And Mrs Thatcher walks behind
 And so does Sailor Ted.

What a blessed relief it was to have a few hours of hot
sunshine after the unnatural cold spell! As if in sympathy with
the public's vote of confidence, the sun came smiling through,
and for the first time this year the Inspector dragged out the
Sunday Telegraph Relaxicouch from the garden shed and
erected it on the sun patio. Harold had soon stretched himself
out in his khaki shorts and openwork sandals to enjoy the
Results on the Yashimoto Portable, a glass of cool Planter's
Knockout Cocktail at his elbow.

'You know, Gladys,' he observed, removing his pipe
from his mouth and letting the fragrant smoke drift upward in
the summer air, 'there are times when it all seems worth it after
all. The country served, one's duty done, a modicum of
appreciation. Poor old Benn! He reminds me of the primitive
Australian Bush Aborigine who first fashioned the boomerang'
— I looked up from darning the Inspector's woolly swim-trunks,
puzzled by his comparison — 'The boomerang is of course the
referendum. He is delighted by his new discovery and, with a
wild gleam in his eye, he launches it skimming into the blue
distance, assured that it will bring home the bacon for his
supper. But no. . . ' Here he broke off his exposition of the
fable, and became convulsed with helpless laughter.
Eventually he contained himself and, wiping the tears from
his eyes with his shirt-tail, refilled his glass from a hotwaterbottle

full of the drink in a bucket of ice under the couch. 'Picture him, Gladys, if you will, a lonely figure in the outback; imagine his consternation as, unseen by him, his man-made bird comes ever closer. And then, WONK! It strikes him on the occiput, stunning him: his eyes cross, and he collapses on the sand, to be sniffed at by hyenas, desert rats and wombats.'

At this his laughter resumed, with such intensity that he did not hear the kitchen door open on the patio and Mr Haines come up behind him in his green baize apron to clear his throat. 'Mr Neave is here, Sir, as arranged,' he soothed. Harold controlled his mirth with a mighty effort of will. 'Neave?' he queried. 'Neave? Neave? Ah yes, I know the fellow. Show him in.' A moment later a quiet gentleman with a briefcase in a sober blazer outfit and striped tie came in to sit down on a plastic covered kitchen stool provided by the Inspector.

'Prime Minister,' he observed, 'this is all rather irregular.' Here he looked dubiously at Mr Haines, who stood expectantly at Harold's elbow. 'Haines, hop it!' snapped Harold. 'Gladys, you understand that this is a private matter. Now, Neave, you do not have to tell me of your patriotic fervour. I am as aware as the next man of how you single-handedly escaped from Colditz, several times.' Here he poured a generous helping of the Planter's Special into one of Giles's blue plastic picnic beakers and handed it to the soberly-dressed gentleman who I took, wrongly as it transpired, to be connected with the Life Insurance business.

'As you know, this country is in deadly peril,' Harold went on. 'Quite so,' Mr Neave spoke out, his chin stuck forward and a strange light gleaming in his eyes as his fingers drummed a ra-ta-tat on the Foldex Gardenware. 'The Reds are massing on our Eastern borders, on shop-floor and in factory, even, if I may say so, on your own back benches. The death-watch beetles are at work in the whole fabric of society.' Overcome with enthusiasm, he then downed the Planter's Knockout at a gulp.
'Now, Neave,' Harold continued to the blenching patriot, swiftly producing the hotwaterbottle to refill his beaker, 'what you say is alas all too true. Tough measures are needed, as they were in the dark days when you and others like you were performing unheard-of feats of valour and gymnastics against the Hun. No, no, do not be modest' — with this he brushed aside a nod of sage agreement from our friend — 'I know I can rely on your chaps to see us through.'

'Well,' Mr Neave said tentatively, straightening his tie and brushing a piece of fluff from his immaculately tailored blazer. 'I'm not quite sure, to be honest, what you're driving at. . . '
'Simply this, Hairy' — I was surprised by this cognomen, but Mr Neave allowed it to pass — 'my crisis package will be fought tooth and nail by those enemies of our country to whom you have so powerfully alluded. It will be up to you and all right-thinking Englishmen to rally to our assistance if it comes to an important scrap. By the way,' and here he refilled his own glass to the brim, 'it is humorous about Benn, is it not, apropos this referendum. I was just saying to Gladys. . . '
Once again he embarked on the lengthy Australian analogy with which he had been so much taken earlier. Mr Neave had hitherto evinced a somewhat wary mien, but now his eyes began to twinkle with real bonhomie and when Harold reached the point where the Aborigine was struck on the back of the head he slapped his thigh and observed, 'Damn good! Damn good! Oh I say! Ha! ha! ha!'

27th JUNE 1975

It is wonderful how, amid all the talk of crisis and show-down, Harold succeeds in maintaining a soignee calm. Wherever he goes, he seems to bring with him an aura of guru-like serenity, though I must confess that being human, there are times when even he 'flips his lid', as the Inspector vividly describes a stress situation.

We were quietly reading the papers at breakfast last Tuesday, the only sound being the Inspector's stolid munching of his Wholegerm Roughage Bricks, when Harold remarked out of the blue: 'You know, Haines, you are looking tired and overworked. Gladys! Do you not notice the pimply pallor of our friend's skin, the bloodshot eyes, the purple bags beneath? Show me your tongue, Haines.' Obediently the factotum opened his mouth. 'There, as I thought. Coated and unpleasant, like the interior of some old kettle. You may close it now. You could, of course, pop round to Doctor Melrose for a check-up, but I can diagnose your trouble easily enough. You have been overdoing it, letting things get on top of you. . . ' At this, the Inspector, who had been examining Mr Haines with distaste, emitted a coarse guffaw. 'You must learn to relax, like the rest of us. Put your feet up. For a start, I suggest you cut out these daily briefings to the Lobby Journalists. Why should you tell them what is going on? Let them earn their money for a change, let them find out for themselves. The processes of government are, after all, a private matter between friends — this is what Dick Crossman failed to realise. It is high time the Press were brought to heel. Why should you devote valuable hours to these people's company when you could be enjoying a frame or two with me down at the Billiard Hall?'

Throughout Harold's harangue I noticed Mr Haines' mood brightening, while a pleasing smile replaced the sulky pout with which he had received the first remarks on his appearance. He was about to speak when Harold looked at his watch and exclaimed, 'Gladys, fetch the Yashimoto, will you — I think you'll find it in the downstairs toilet — it is just approaching half past eight and time to listen in to the new experimental broadcasts from the House of Commons.'

I found the transistor and, sure enough, as we turned it on, Mr Short's voice came through in ringing tones. 'This is just the nuts and bolts of parliamentary business, of course,' Harold prompted, arranging his feet on the table and settling down to listen. 'I think it is important that the listeners should be able to hear for themselves how the ancient traditions of the Mother of Parliaments are observed. But listen to this bit coming now! Inspector, stop munching, if you please! Now, absolutely quiet!'

As we leaned forward eagerly to catch each intonation, I could not but be reminded of the wartime days when, as a Land Girl, I listened to the heroic words of Mr Winston Churchill, as he then was, telling us all about the fighting on the beaches. 'Is the Prime Minister aware', the curious fluting tones of Mrs Thatcher could be heard to ask, 'of the grave economic crisis that is threatening us here today? We see unemployment at a record figure, we see the pound slipping, and what is the Prime Minister going to do? That is what we want to know.' There was a momentary pause as Harold could be heard rising to his feet. 'I have seen the Gallup Poll today in the *Daily Telegraph*, if that is what you mean. "Do you or do you not think that Mrs Thatcher is doing a good job as Leader of the Opposition?" and I quote from paragraph fifteen of column three: "Yes 23%, No 48%". . . ' Without emotion, Mrs Thatcher gallantly pursued her question. 'What steps is the Prime Minister going to take to control the runaway inflation that is daily growing more and more runaway?'
'Two months ago,' Harold countered, quick as a flash, 'in the same newspaper, "Yes 53%". Heh! Heh! Heh! You are not doing very well, are you? You are trying to get your popularity back asking me these questions, aren't you?' At this, the announcer broke in to introduce a lengthy monologue by Mr Clement Freud advertising dog food, and Harold scowled angrily. 'I knew this would happen. They've cut the punch line. Haines, ring the BBC this minute: the whole routine, the timing, everything is ruined by this kind of insensitive editing. There was a big laugh in there, building to applause. These editors are butchers. They have no sense of artistic integrity. Ring up Sir Charles Curran at once. If necessary I shall have to edit the thing myself. The ratings will be through the floor unless a show like this is professionally presented.'

After Harold had gone, the Inspector continued his readings from the Lucan case. I have found the whole story curiously moving, as has Sir John, who said on the phone this morning that it had an Edwardian charm all of its own. I myself have experienced a deep sympathy for the lonely, wide-eyed figure of Lady Lucan, shackled for life to an inveterate gambler.

Goodness me, this sweltering weather goes on and on.
I expect that in years to come we will look back on 1975 as our
grandparents did on the golden era of the long hot Edwardian
garden party when Lady Asquith whirled in the arms of
Lytton Strachey to some popular waltz by Sir Edward Elgar.

These thoughts passed through my mind as Harold and I
strolled through the floats and engineering displays at the
Royal Agricultural Festival Heavy Implements Show at
Stoatbury-on-Trim, Worcs., and were issued, for the benefit
of photographers, with delightful plastic punnets of
Captain Mark Phillips Brand soya-extract simulated strawberries
with recycled cream. Then Harold made his speech, emphasising
that there was to be no panic, while the Stoatbury Young
Farmers Silver Band played a selection from Sibelius'
Titanic Suite.

'Ladies and Gentlemen,' Harold soothed, his silver hair
momentarily wafted by a light summer breeze, 'the parrot cry
of the Cocktail Belt is braying for panic measures.'
At this a messenger came running in, and attempted to force
his way through the plump yeomen listening to the snatches
of Harold's speech which were audible in the quieter passages
of the music. 'But us down here in Worcs. have our feet on the
ground: we are not easily thrown off balance by every wind
that blows.' By now the messenger had at last reached the
podium, and handed a telegram up to Harold who opened it,
and with a strangled cry plunged out of view behind the bank
of potted Granny Goodman Dwarf Apple Trees. A moment
later Mr Haines was at my side and ushered me through the
glazed audience as the band played on, apparently oblivious
of Harold's sudden departure.

Harold's mood, as Mr Haines and Lady Forkbender climbed
into the front of the Mini, was more disturbed than I have seen
it for many years. His face was pale, and beads of sweat stood out
upon his brow. 'Step on it, Haines!' he cried in desperate tones.
'The Pound is at its lowest ever and still plummeting! I must get
back to restore confidence!' He sat staring wild-eyed and
chewed his finger-nails, until Lady Forkbender brought a phial
of capsules out of her handbag and passed one to him,

saying that she always used them when things got on top of her.

Whatever the palliative, it appeared to have a marked effect
on Harold, and when we reached the outskirts of Swindon,
he insisted on Mr Haines making a long detour to visit a public
house called *The Sputnik Lounge*, where we were all able to sit
outside between the toilets and the garage, while Harold quaffed
a Jumbo of Malt Drain's Four Star Executive Special,
ignoring Lady Forkbender's warning that he should not drink
on top of one of the pills. After a brief altercation, during which
Lady Forkbender became highly distressed and began to tremble,
Harold sent Haines back into the Lounge to buy another round
of drinks, while Lady Forkbender rose to her feet and
ostentatiously went inside to play the pinball machine.

Mr Haines returned with the drinks on a tin tray and
intimated that we must soon be getting along as Mr Healey was
waiting for him at Number Eleven with the foreign bankers.
Harold gazed at him for some time with a beaming smile,
and then took a long swig of the Executive Drink which left
a moustache-like crust of white foam on his upper lip.
'Haines,' he remarked. 'Here is Ten p. Ring Denis, there's a good
chap, and tell him that I do not believe in interfering with the
day-to-day problems of my Ministers. He must do as he sees fit.'

Later in the afternoon, we stopped by an abandoned
gravel pit near Slough, and Harold insisted that Mr Haines
should accompany him for a swim in their drawers.
Lady Forkbender remained sitting in the car, reading a magazine
called *Cosmopolitan*. Harold came out first, easing his
flannelette underpants and lying down beside me on the grit.
'You know, Gladys,' he observed, closing his eyes and turning
his face towards the benevolent beams of hot summer sun,
'when you have been through two or three Sterling crises,
it doesn't have the same excitement any more somehow.
It's all new to Denis; he will enjoy it. I expect they'll cook up
some wages thing for him to sign from Zurich. Foot and Benn
will make a bit of a fuss, but they'll stay on. The Unions won't
take a blind bit of notice, with any luck it'll be at least three
months before. . . '

His voice trailed away, and soon a rhythmic snoring
informed me that he had gone to sleep.

'Tis told that once in days gone by
  On the banks of the Zuyder Zee
There dwelt a Dutch boy, blond and shy
  Who lived with his family

One day, Hans Brinkman — 'twas his name —
  Was walking along by the dyke
A merry song from his lips there came
  As he went on his happy hike

But lo, all in that summer day
  The thunderclouds gathered above
And the rain splashed down all cold and grey
  Drenching both cow and dove

O horrors! What is this he sees?
  A hole has appeared in the wall!
And as the hurricane bends the trees
  Out springs a waterfall

Shall all old Holland's land be drowned?
  The tulips and windmills and clogs
Shall the cruel sea foam all around
  Where once lay slumbering hogs?

'No, it shall not, it shall not be'
  Up spoke the little Dutch tyke
Thrusting his finger courageously
  Into the crumbling dyke

So all was saved: and so today
  As inflation threatens our land
Brave Harold's finger points the way
  Alone behold him stand:

Six pounds and not a penny more!
  The tumultuous waves roll back
Fair peace returns to field and shore
  Let's hope he will not crack.

'Well, that's it,' Harold remarked on Monday morning, opening the upstairs cupboard to get his khaki shorts and clock golf set out for our holidays in the Scilly Isles. 'That has sewn it up for the time being anyway. The Unions are toeing the line, the bosses have come to heel, the Gnomes are satisfied. You may ask,' he continued, blowing the dust off his rubber flippers and snorkel kit, 'where are the tributes from the media? Where is the recognition of a grateful country? You look of course in vain.'

With this he climbed on a rickety chair to extract Giles's somewhat perished RAF-style mountain rescue inflatable dinghy from its place above the water tank. 'The days are gone when I expected plaudits. As Shakespeare said, a prophet is more popular abroad than he is at home. Gladys, what have you done with my espadrilles? I expect you gave them to Lady Longford's Bring and Buy for Mentally Distressed Gentlefolk.'

Harold was outside loading the Mini prior to our departure, and I was busy with the Tupperware Superseal Salad Box, when a confused shouting and tramping of feet could be heard coming down Lord North Street. I ran out to find Harold, a cigar in one hand and a bottle of Wincola Fortified Car Drink in the other, staring in consternation at an advancing column, accompanied by a police escort, of shouting men, their clothes in disarray, and many of them singing raucously. At the head of the procession, a large banner floated in the air, bearing the legend: 'We're on the Boyle — Labour MPs Want Cash Now'. Pausing only a moment to shut the car boot, Harold ran into the house and slammed the door, calling through the keyhole that I was to inform the MPs he had gone to Strasbourg.

A moment later, like someone at a football match, I was engulfed in a struggling mob of Members of Parliament, some of them smelling strongly of drink, who wedged me against the front door and seemed ready to stop at nothing. Just as I thought my end had come, I felt the front door yield behind me, and the Inspector's strong left arm pulled me to safety while his right, equipped with his burglar's friend, dealt a few sharp blows to the bald pates of the ringleaders. 'Phew!' he remarked as we stood panting in the hall. 'That was a narrow shave. As ugly a bunch as it has been my fortune to see Madam, since my days in Limehouse.'

Thunderous blows continued to fall on the front door, and the tinkle of glass announced that we could not hope to hold out long. In the kitchen I found Harold on the telephone, summoning his Deputy Leader. The street was up for some repairs at the front of the house, he said, so could Mr Short come round via the back garden as soon as possible.

It seemed an age before the grey-haired figure of the former headmaster could be seen dropping nimbly over the wall and picking his way through the flowerbed.
Harold was on hand to greet him, and made light of the raucous background din which was all too clearly audible through the closed door of the kitchen. 'These workmen are high-spirited chaps, many of them from Ireland and the West Indies,' he remarked in casual tones. 'Now, Short, I have to go to Brussels for talks with whatever number it is of our Common Market counterparts, and I am leaving you in charge. There is nothing very urgent, I think' — at this moment a brick flew through the window in the front hall, striking the grandfather clock and causing it to chime continuously for twenty-four strokes — 'so I can leave it in your hands.'

'Just one moment, Prime Minister,' interposed the erstwhile pedagogue, unwrapping the Funsize chocolate Breakthrough Bar that I had offered him. 'The question of Members' salaries. It may look bad for us if we give way on the full amount whilst others are being urged to exercise restraint.' 'Indeed,' Harold replied, raising his voice slightly against the growing noise, 'I am sure that all Members, at least on our side of the House, will appreciate the need to set an example at this crucial moment in our nation's history. Anyway, I know that you will handle it with your habitual aplomb. And now let me show you out.'

Still eating his Breakthrough, Mr Short allowed himself to be propelled forward through the hall and out of the front door. We had a momentary glimpse of flushed faces, and heard a savage roar as Mr Short was swallowed up in the throng. Then the door slammed to, and Harold put the bolt and chain across.
'As an ex-schoolmaster,' he observed wryly, 'Short knows how to deal with hooligans.' Consulting his watch he added, 'The pubs will be opening again in half an hour, and our boisterous friends will doubtless then disperse. Tell Haines to bring the Lilo and my *Reader's Digest Book of Seaside Walks* from the Den. I think the time has come to get away.'